LOCOMOTIVES

LOCOMOTIVES

FROM THE
STEAM LOCOMOTIVE
TO THE
BULLET TRAIN
TIM FREW

MALLARD PRESS

An Imprint of BDD Promotional Book Company, Inc.
666 Fifth Avenue
New York, New York 10103

A FRIEDMAN GROUP BOOK

Published by MALLARD PRESS
An imprint of BDD Promotional Book Company, Inc.
666 Fifth Avenue
New York, New York 10103

ISBN 0-792-45260-7

LOCOMOTIVES: From the Steam Locomotive to the Bullet Train
was prepared and produced by
Michael Friedman Publishing Group, Inc.
15 West 26th Street
New York, New York 10010

Editors: Sharon Kalman and Sharyn Rosart
Art Director: Jeff Batzli
Designer: Robert W. Kosturko
Photography Editor: Christopher Bain
Production: Karen L. Greenberg

Typeset by: BPE Graphics
Color separations by United South Sea Graphic Art Co., Ltd.
Printed and bound in Hong Kong by Leefung-Asco Printers Ltd.

The publisher wishes to acknowledge that extensive attempts have
been made to contact the holders of the copyrights on all artwork
in this volume; we apologize for any errors or missing credits.

Dedication
To my parents, Bill and Evie.

Acknowledgments
I would like to thank everyone at the Michael Friedman Publishing
Group who had a hand in this project: my editors, Sharyn Rosart and
Sharon Kalman, for their patience with me; the designer, Bob Kosturko,
for his artistic ability; the photography editors Christopher Bain
and Daniella Jo Nilva for their knack in finding the right photo;
and, finally, the production team, Karen Greenberg and Marc Sapir,
the two who keep the ball rolling, yet seldom get acknowledged.

C O N T E N T S

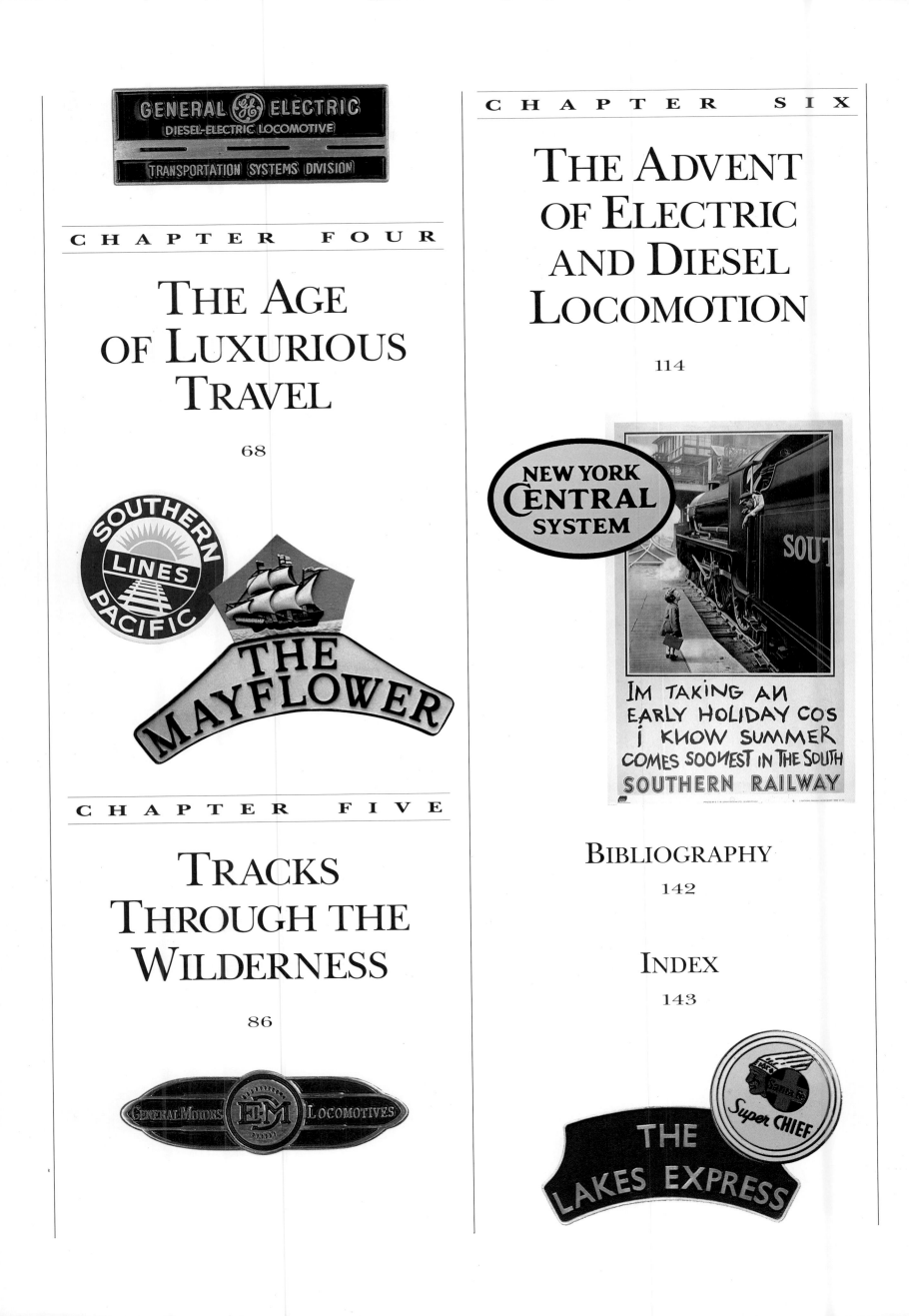

INTRODUCTION

ON SEPTEMBER 17, 1825, GEORGE STEPHENSON drove a steam-powered train named the *Locomotion* down the newly completed Stockton & Darlington Railway in England, the first mechanized public railroad. That first, largely unheralded, trip marked the beginning of a transportation revolution that forever changed the history of the world. Throughout the rest of the nineteenth and early twentieth centuries the steam locomotive was the chief driving force of the Industrial Revolution. The completion of a transcontinental railroad helped to reunite the young, war-stricken United States; in Russia, the Trans-Siberian railroad opened up a resource-rich wilderness; and many historians equate the history of the Dominion of Canada with the history of the Canadian Pacific Railroad.

In the middle years of the twentieth century, the railroads converted from steam power to electric power to diesel power, and then back to electric power, in an attempt to effectively compete with the airplane and the automobile. Most recently, the railroad industry has developed high-speed electric passenger trains as a last-ditch effort to keep this mode of transportation alive. While the railroads will never completely die, their years of transportation dominance are nevertheless long gone.

The history of the world's railroads is so far reaching that no single volume can hope to do justice to the subject. This book only skims the surface of the rich and fascinating story of the railroads. By reading these pages and scanning the photos you will become more aware of the lasting impact of locomotive.

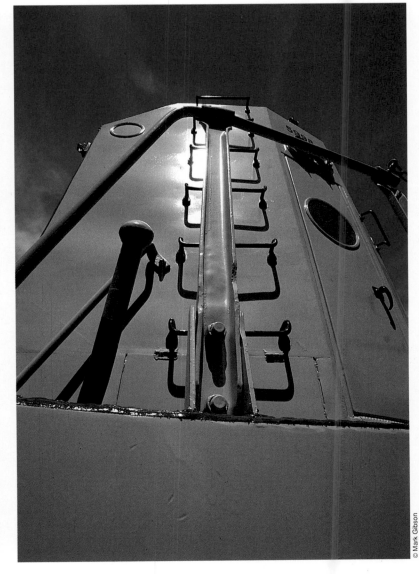

THE ROAD TO LOCOMOTION

AROUND 200 B.C., HERO OF ALEXANDRIA, A GREEK mathematician and physicist, completed a book examining machines and devices that harnessed water and air power. Written nearly two thousand years before the first steam locomotive puffed and chugged its way across a tramway in South Wales, Hero's *Spiritalia seu Pneumatica* described one such machine that used steam to create motion.

Named the aeolipile in honor of Aeolius, the Greek god of the winds, Hero's curious-looking device consisted of a caldron with a tight-fitting lid, on top of which were two hollow, ornate columns supporting a hollow sphere that held two right-angled exhaust pipes placed 180 degrees apart. When water was heated in the caldron, steam rose through the columns and into the sphere. The steam would then exit through the exhaust pipes, causing the sphere to spin.

This device, and other similar ones, fast became the scientific curiosities of the gentry. Noble houses across Europe soon owned some version of the aeolipile. These machines, however, were built solely for amusement. It would be centuries before spirited inventors discovered a way to harness

FPG International

FPG International

FPG International

Legend states that when James Watt was a young boy, he took one look at his mother's teakettle and proclaimed, "Some day I shall invent the world's first steam-powered engine." While he was not really the "father of the steam engine," as he was later dubbed, Watt did make several significant improvements on the designs of earlier inventors.

the power of steam for any practical purposes.

In the early seventeenth century, an Italian named Giovanni Branca invented what was later to be recognized as the first impulse turbine. The boiler for his strange machine was cast in the form of a bust of a cigar-smoking Indian. Water was boiled in the torso, causing steam to fill the head and escape through the cigar-shaped tube protruding from the lips. The escaping jets of steam turned a miniature windmill supported by two columns. Through a series of reduction gears, Branca was able to convert the velocity of the windmill into power and thereby move two cams, which in turn raised and lowered a pair of pestles into two mortar bowls.

While this machine still fell into the category of scientific curiosity, Branca envisioned larger models being used to operate water pumps. At this time, there was a growing demand for coal and ore and, as a result, a sharp increase in mining. Manually operated piston pumps were widely used to pump wa-

ter out of the deep mines. Branca's machine, however, was not efficient enough to effectively power a large mining pump.

It was not until the beginning of the eighteenth century that Thomas Newcomen, an Englishman, first found a practical way to operate a piston pump with steam power. He achieved this by attaching a second, steam-driven piston to a water piston. He would then alternately direct vapor in and out of the steam piston, using it to drive the water piston.

Newcomen built his first two-story pumping station in England in 1705. The operation of this oak, iron, and brick "atmospheric engine" involved opening a valve that sent steam into an upright cylinder. At the top of the cylinder a large, raised piston was attached to a second pumping piston by means of a walking board. When the cylinder was full, the operator shut off the steam valve and opened a second valve that let cold water pour over the outer surface of the hot cylinder. As the cylinder cooled, the steam inside it condensed, creating a vacuum. The air pressure outside then drove the piston down, raising the opposite end of the walking beam, thus pumping the water from the mine below.

Newcomen hired a young man named Humphrey Potter to operate the machine. The inventive Potter soon grew tired of the tedious job of opening and closing the valves four times a minute, so he devised a system of ropes that, when attached to the walking beam, would open and close the valves automatically. Potter's modifications were so effective that his job became obsolete.

Any great discovery consists of two parts inventiveness and one part accident. Such is the case with the atmospheric engine. Soon after Newcomen began operating his new pumping station at full force, a broken valve began to leak cooling water directly into the steam cylinder. Much to everyone's surprise, this "mechanical defect" proved most rewarding. The incursion of this cooling water sped up the condensation process, causing the piston to rise and fall six times a minute instead of the usual four. Newcomen quickly redesigned his cylinder with a cooling pipe running directly into the cylinder.

The atmospheric engine was such a success that similar engines were built across England and the European continent. In 1763, a model of Newcomen's pump fell into the hands of mathematical instrument maker James Watt. Legend states that Watt, who was later dubbed father of the steam engine, looked at his mother's teakettle one day and proclaimed: "Some day I shall invent the world's first steam engine." The father of the steam engine he was not, but Watt did bring many revolutionary improvements to Newcomen's design.

Through meticulous experimentation, Watt greatly increased the steam piston engine's fuel efficiency and speed. He developed the first closed, double-acting cylinder. In this design, steam was alternately released into two ends of a closed cylinder, thereby bringing power to both strokes of the piston. Newcomen's design relied on outside air pressure for a single, downward thrust. In addition, Watt invented the fly-ball governor, which used levers and centrifugal force to control the speed of the engine. Watt further improved the steam engine's efficiency through the use of a double-chambered boiler for condensing the steam.

While Watt's reputation for expertise in the area of steam engines grew along with the popularity of his pumpers, he remained loyal to the notion that steam-powered vehicles were as impractical as the high-pressure steam engine that would be needed to propel

Improvements such as the double-chambered boiler and the closed, double-action cylinder greatly enhanced the power and efficiency of Watt's engines. His pumpers quickly became famous across England; however, Watt never believed the steam engine could be used to propel a vehicle.

Despite the criticisms of skeptics such as James Watt, determined inventors such as Nicholas Cugnot and William Murdock built and tested crude steam-powered vehicles. This model of an early steam vehicle was based on the drawings and notes of Isaac Newton.

them. The noted journalist Zerah Colburn once wrote of the so-called father of the steam engine, "no one man did more in his way to retard the development of the locomotive." In the meantime, many resourceful inventors were hard at work, trying to prove Watt wrong.

Early Steam-Powered Vehicles

In 1769, the French war minister, the Duke of Choiseul, under the authority of Louis XV, commissioned inventor Nicholas Cugnot to put together a steam tractor for hauling heavy cannons and artillery pieces. The resultant steam tricycle's massive frame was supported by three thick wheels, two in the rear and one in the front. The front driving wheel was powered by two steam pistons and a large copper boiler-firebox that hung out over the front of the apparatus.

The puffing, snorting machine proved far from practical as it chugged and lurched its way along the streets of Paris at a blazing two miles (three kilometers) an hour. While it did possess enough power to pull the heavy nine-ton (eight-metric-ton) cannons, Cugnot's steam tractor came to a grinding halt every

ten minutes and had to be fed a fresh supply of wood and water. Moreover, the three-wheeled design made turning rather precarious. One day, an artillery man who had the misfortune of being ordered to drive the smoke-spewing beast tried to cut a corner too sharply, and flipped the machine onto its side. He escaped safely, but steam and embers exploded from the hot boiler, spreading fire and mayhem across a normally peaceful French neighborhood.

Across the channel in England, a talented young engineer named William Murdoch was making progress on a steam-powered carriage of his own. Hired as an assistant to James Watt, Murdoch did not subscribe to his mentor's short-sighted notions on the future of steam power. Upon discovering that Murdoch was devoting hours to developing a road vehicle powered by a high-pressure engine, Watt tried to have Murdoch fired. Fortunately for Murdoch, he was employed not by Watt but by the Birmingham plant that produced the Watt pumpers.

Despite Watt's interference, Murdoch was able to finish a small, working model of a steam locomotive. This miniature tricycle used a small boiler heated by an oil lamp. The cylinder and piston powered a hinged beam that raised and lowered a rod connected to a crank on the rear axle.

American Association of Railroads

North Wind Picture Archives

Legend states that Murdoch tested his invention at night to avoid the ridicule of James Watt. One night, a vicar was entertaining a young lady outside his home on the same street. When the tiny steam tricycle careened down the lane, the vicar saw it as an angry sign from God and ran off, leaving poor Murdoch to comfort the young lady. Despite the small success of the tiny tricycle, and the adventure that accompanied it, Murdoch abandoned the project and went on to invent the coal-gas lamp.

Over the next 100 years, many others tried their hand at building workable, steam-powered road machines, all with varying degrees of success and failure. It became evident that the country roads, city streets, and even the new turnpikes, springing up all over England and the continent, were still too rough for the fragile steam engine. A working prototype would steam along fine until it landed in an unseen hole or gully, resulting in a volcanic eruption of steam and glowing embers that caused the driver and any bystanders to run frantically for cover.

A solution to this problem was found in the beginning of the nineteenth century. Horse-powered railways, tramways, and plateways sprung up all over England to aid in the transport of goods and raw materials that helped feed the then burgeoning Industrial Revolution. It wasn't long before a few forward-thinking men realized the great potential of combining a steam engine with an iron rail.

Why The Railways Came

In the late eighteenth and early nineteenth centuries, England and Europe were undergoing a transformation that would have a more profound and everlasting impact than any other in the history of Western civilization. The Industrial Revolution not only changed the economic structure of Europe but also radically altered its age-old social structure. The old feudal system of aristocracy and peasant was rapidly vanishing.

Ironically enough, the new methods of agriculture, which created a dependable supply of food for industrial workers and the rapidly growing population, were a major contributor to the Industrial Revolution. A new industrial middle class was born, and along with this new economic structure there emerged hundreds of towns and cities, providing markets for manufactured goods. With all of the major prerequisites for industrialization—a steady food supply, a growing population, expanding world trade, resourceful inventors, a supply of coal and metal ores for heavy industry, and, above all, a new system of roads and canals to transport goods—England led the Industrial Revolution.

England was searching for new and better ways to transport goods to and from its blossoming industrial centers. The road and highway systems were slow, crowded, and difficult to maintain and were often the scene of increasingly violent "highway robberies." The canals, although quicker and somewhat safer,

As the Industrial Revolution swept across Europe, there grew an increasing demand for a new and faster form of transportation. England led the way by building a complex network of canals, highways, and horse-powered tramways.

21

In 1803, Samuel Homfray made a 500-guinea wager that a steam-powered vehicle could pull ten tons of iron the entire length of the nine-mile Pen-y-Darran railway. To make good on his wager, Homfray hired Richard Trevithick (right) to develop a steam vehicle that could travel on rails. Although Trevithick's locomotive was crude, it successfully answered the now famous Pen-y-Darran Challenge.

were limited to the range of natural water-ways and, thus, impossible for extensive land travel. In addition, manufacturers grew tired of the monopolistic attitude of the canal owners—for, along with industrialization and economic growth, came greed.

By the beginning of the nineteenth century, a third transportation alternative was being put into widespread use—horse- or man-powered tramways and railways. Metal or wood rail lines were laid down around collieries across England. By reducing friction and increasing the load possibilities, these railways made the horse more efficient. Horse-rail haulage had been used in Europe since the late sixteenth century, but it was limited to private use and carrying heavy loads over very short distances.

In 1803, the first public horse-drawn freight railway was opened, the Surrey Iron Railway, which ran from Croydon to Wandsworth; four years later the first public passenger railway, the Swansea and Mumbles, was opened. These two railways opened the door for the creation of several more public railways in England and a few on the European continent. As successful as these may have been, they were hampered by the same problem as the canals and the highways—they were limited by the efficiency of the horse.

Richard Trevithick and The Pen-y-Darran Challenge

One of the most successful and widely used of the horse-drawn railways was the Pen-y-Darran, which transported freight from the Pen-y-Darran ironworks to Merthyr Tydfil nine miles (fourteen kilometers) away. One afternoon in 1803, Samuel Homfray, an officer at the ironworks, commented to a few of his associates that someday the steam carriage would take the place of the horse in hauling heavy freight. Homfray was chided and ridiculed by the others at the impracticality of such a prospect. At the time, the steam carriage was a novelty that few had seen or heard of except Homfray, who had seen it at an exhibition in London.

Holding a substantial pecuniary interest in the patent rights to the high-pressure steam engine, Homfray was both financially and intellectually intrigued by the prospect of a steam-driven locomotive. As a result, he soon found himself wagering 500 guineas with the most boisterous of his critics that ten tons (nine metric tons) of iron could be moved the

Many early inventors set up exhibitions in order to raise interest and money for their projects. This early drawing depicts Richard Trevithick demonstrating one of his locomotives in 1808.

entire length of the Pen-y-Darran line under the power of steam alone. To devise such a contraption, Homfray turned to Richard Trevithick, whom Homfray had hired to build a stationary steam engine for the plant's rolling mill. Not so coincidentally, Trevithick was also the inventor of the steam carriage Homfray had seen exhibited in London earlier that year.

Cornishman Richard Trevithick was a resourceful inventor and amateur wrestler whose brawn was outdone only by his brains. Trevithick's first major contribution to steam locomotion came in 1800, when he developed the first practical high-pressure engine. An immense improvement over Watt's stationary engine, Trevithick's machine was powerful enough and light enough to carry itself under its own power. Trevithick first applied his new engine to road transport at Camborne, Cornwall, on Christmas Eve, 1801. The steam carriage was faster than walking; yet, it was unable to negotiate hills and soon broke down.

He demonstrated his newest model in London in 1803. This carriage ran at nine miles (fourteen kilometers) an hour, but was unable to withstand the constant jarring and rocking caused by the primitive roads. Together, Trevithick and Homfray worked to try to mate the sensitive steam engine with the smooth surface of a metal railway.

On February 13, 1804, the strange-looking contraption was readied for its first run.

Weighing more than 11,000 pounds (4,100 kilograms), Trevithick's locomotive was powered by a five-foot (two-meter), horizontal boiler and a four-and-a-half foot (1.3-meter) piston stroke. A flywheel, crank, and gear-combination transferred the power to the fifty-two-inch (1.3-meter) drive wheels.

Homfray won his wager, as the engine carried its ten-ton (nine-metric-ton) load the prescribed nine miles (fourteen kilometers) to Merthyr Tydfil in a little more than two hours. According to a Bristol newspaper covering the historic event, the engine "was made use of to convey along the tram road 10 tons' (nine metric tons) weight of bar iron from Pen-y-Darran ironworks to the place where it joins the Glamorganshire canal, upwards of nine miles distant; and it is necessary to observe that the weight of the load was soon increased from ten to fifteen tons by about seventy persons riding on the trams, who, drawn thither (as well as many hundreds of others) by invincible curiosity, were eager to ride.... The engine performed the journey without feeding the boiler or using any water, and will travel with ease at the rate of five miles an hour."

The engine, however, was too heavy for the early track, and left a mass of twisted and broken plates and rails in its wake. While the experiment was not a complete success, it did prove that smooth wheels on a smooth track could carry an extremely heavy payload. A

*Adhesion (the ability of a smooth wheel to pull on a smooth track) was a major obstacle confronting the early developers of the steam locomotive. Many strange contraptions, such as the **Mechanical Traveler** (right) were invented in the hope of solving this problem. One of the earliest successes was the **Puffing Billy** (below), built by William Hedley and Timothy Hackworth for the Wylam colliery in 1813.*

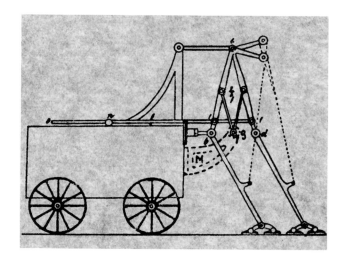

practical locomotive did not seem far away. The final hurdle was to develop a machine that was heavy enough to retain the needed traction, yet light enough so that it wouldn't destroy the track.

In the years that followed, several bizarre prototypes were tested with varying degrees of success. The most unusual machine built during this time was the *Mechanical Traveler*. Developed by William Burton in 1813, this engine literally walked along the track. Propelled by two mechanical legs that pushed it from behind, the *Mechanical Traveler* was clocked at speeds in excess of three miles

(five kilometers) an hour. It was relatively light and seemed to solve the traction problem, but it could not withstand the constant pounding of its propulsion system. More than one head must have turned on the day of its last run, when this great mechanical grasshopper reared up and caused an explosion that showered the track with steaming water, glowing embers, and mechanical limbs.

The first successful locomotive to solve the traction problem came in 1811 from John Blenkinsop and Matthew Murray at the Middleton Colliery near Leeds. This cog railway system used an engine whose steam-powered cog wheel engaged a toothed-rack rail that was added to a normal track. This cog railway eliminated slippage, but installation was very costly. While only a few of these locomotives were ever used, the cog system later proved its worth on sharply inclined railways across the world.

These "improvements" and others floundered until William Hedley and Timothy Hackworth, a blacksmith, introduced the *Puffing Billy* in 1814. Working from a model of Trevithick's locomotive, they combined it with the best innovations from several sources. They used a slightly improved version of Trevithick's boiler; a two-cylinder system

Another answer to the adhesion problem was Blenkinsop's rack locomotive (left). It wasn't, however, until a thirty-one-year-old engine-wright named George Stephenson (below) turned his attention to the railways that the steam-powered locomotive became a viable form of transportation.

adapted from the work of Murdoch and Cugnot (this eliminated the need for a flywheel); a rocking beam driving arrangement similar to that used on Murdoch's tricycle; and a complex gear drive (similar to Trevithick's) to apply power to all four wheels. This last innovation, spreading the driving force to four wheels instead of two, provided better traction and exerted less stress on the track. Both the *Puffing Billy* and its successor, the *Wylam Dilly,* were eventually rebuilt with eight wheels to further decrease damage to the track.

While these machines succeeded as short-line freight haulers, their complex gearing and long piston strokes made them slow and impractical for long haul freight and passenger service. And even on the short haul, most collieries preferred the use of stationary steam engines that pulled wagons by means of a cable. One man, however, did have the insight and determination to transform these crude colliery engines into a revolutionary means of public transportation.

George Stephenson and The Darlington & Stockton Railway

George Stephenson, generally considered the father of the modern railway, was a self-taught man who grew up along the Wylam tramroad and eventually worked at the Killingworth Colliery on the Tyne. At thirty-one, when he

was an engine-wright at the colliery, he became obsessed with the possibilities of steam locomotion.

Stephenson persuaded mine owner Lord Ravensworth to finance his experimentation. With a modest shop, plenty of financial backing, and only limited experience, Stephenson went to work on improving the design of the *Puffing Billy* and other contemporary steam engines. He completed his first engine, *The Blucher* (named after the allied Prussian general) by 1814. While this primitive engine was hardly an improvement over other engines of

American Association of Railroads

American Association of Railroads

The first steam locomotive built by George Stephenson was the **Blucher** *(right). By simplifying the complicated gear-drive system of the* **Puffing Billy,** *Stephenson was able to attain greater speeds with fewer breakdowns. Above is the "first known picture of a railroad," originally published in 1812. Stephenson later improved upon the* **Blucher** *design with the* **Locomotion,** *which he developed for use on the Stockton and Darlington Railway.*

the time, it made Stephenson aware of the many engineering problems of building a steam locomotive. Stephenson continued to produce engines, and with each new one he simplified and streamlined his mechanics.

Throughout this process of simplification, Stephenson made revolutionary advancements in steam technology. He discovered that a narrow chimney would create a faster draft and a more intense heat in the furnace. In addition, he mounted the cylinders on top of the boiler to simplify the mechanical drive, resulting in less power loss. Stephenson's most significant advancement came when he examined the complicated gear-drive system of the *Puffing Billy*. Finding that this system was the source of many mechanical break-

downs and severely cut the engine's speed potential, he developed a simple arrangement of connecting rods and crank pins, which remained the standard for all steam locomotives to come.

Stephenson's big break came when he met a Quaker financier named Edward Pease. Pease headed a group of coal mine owners and merchants who had discovered that building a canal was too costly and were looking into the possibility of building a horse-powered public tramway for "the conveyance of coal, iron, lime, corn, and other commodities from the interior of the county of Durham to the town of Darlington and the town and port of Stockton."

Stephenson met with Pease on the day the Darlington Railway Act was approved, legalizing the Darlington to Stockton Railroad. Impressed by Stephenson's enthusiasm and determination, Pease hired the engineering prodigy and agreed to his advice that iron rails should be built instead of the wooden tramway originally planned. More important, Stephenson also convinced Pease that at least part, if not all, of the railway should be worked by steam locomotives. Pease was so enamored of Stephenson that he agreed to finance the Robert Stephenson & Company locomotive works (named after George's son and coworker) at Newcastle-upon-Tyne. While several of the investors were confident that steam traction would work on their railway, many others were not. A compromise was worked out where the railway would be run with a combination of steam locomotion, horse power, and rope haulage with stationary steam engines.

On September 27, 1825, the *Locomotion*, driven by George Stephenson, steamed through a triumphant grand opening of the Stockton & Darlington Railway. One newspaper account of the event read: "The engine started off, drawing six loaded wagons, a passenger carriage, and twenty-one trucks fitted with seats. Such was the velocity that in some parts the speed was twelve miles an hour. The number of passengers was counted to be 450, which with coals and other things, would amount to nearly thirty tons. The engine and its load did the first journey of eight and three-quarter miles in five minutes over an hour."

The new railway was quite profitable and soon gained the attention of investors throughout England, Europe, and the United States. The Stockton & Darlington was a success, and George Stephenson was its mastermind. His association with the first steam-operated public railway assured his place in history and opened the door to a much more difficult and ambitious undertaking: laying thirty-five miles (fifty-six kilometers) of track between the textile city of Manchester and the nearest seaport, Liverpool. The modern age of the railway was about to begin.

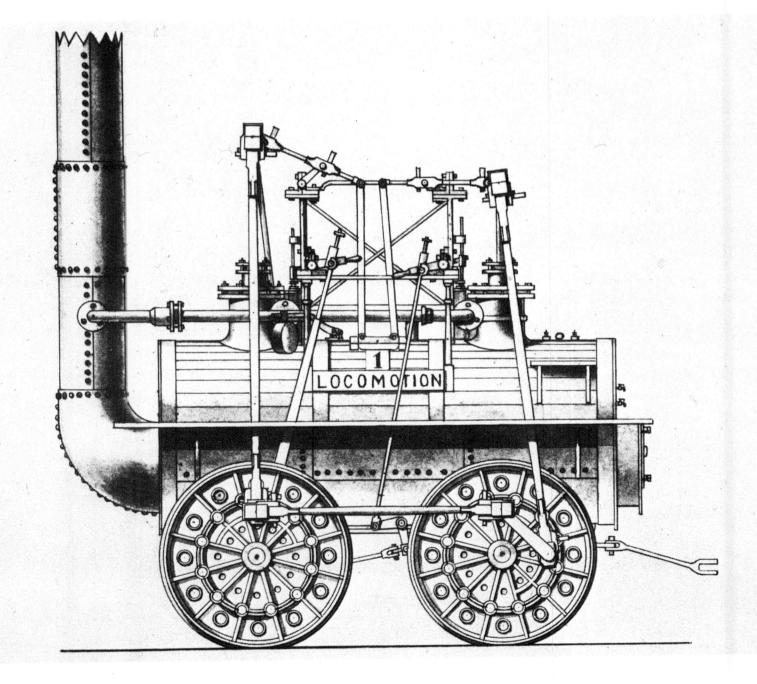

National Railway Museum/York, England

27

THE BIRTH OF THE MODERN RAILWAY

THE GRAND OPENING OF THE LIVERPOOL AND MAN-chester Railway on September 15, 1830, marked the beginning of the modern railway age. This was the first public railway to possess all the basic characteristics of a modern rail system: a double track of iron rails used to transport passengers and freight; complete steam locomotive drive; a system of stations, signals, bridges, and tunnels; and even three different classes of carriages. Actually, three other steam-powered public railways preceded the L&M by a few years: the Stockton & Darlington (1825), the Bolton & Leigh (1828), and the Canterbury & Whitstable (1830). Both the Stockton & Darlington and the Bolton & Leigh, however, were powered by a combination of steam locomotive, stationary steam engine with rope haulage, and horse-drawn wagons. Moreover, the Bolton & Leigh, though it opened in 1828, didn't become truly operational until 1831. The Canterbury & Whitstable, on the other hand, was a fully steam-powered line built by George Stephenson's son Robert; it was mainly used in building the Liverpool & Manchester.

The L&MR was the brainchild of a group of Liverpudlian

The famous Rainhill Trials were held October 1829 in order to find the best locomotive for the new Liverpool and Manchester Railway. The **Sans Pareil,** *entered by Timothy Hackworth, was the fastest and most powerful locomotive in the contest.*

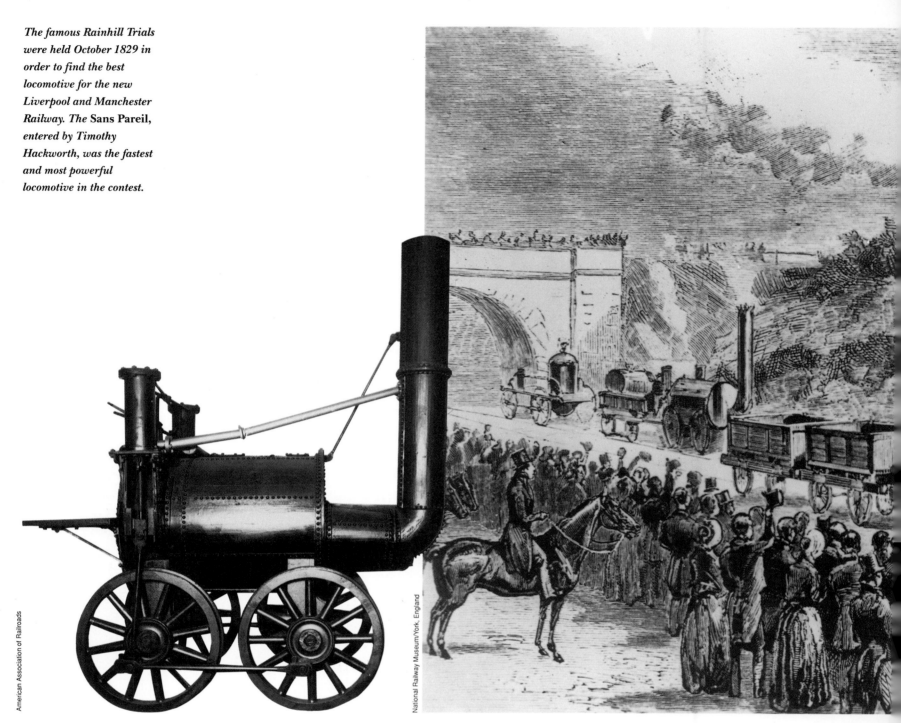

financiers and merchants headed by Joseph Sandars and Henry Booth. Incensed by the high prices and poor service of the monopolistic canal companies, these men were looking for an alternative system of transportation. They turned to William James of Henley-in-Arden, a self-proclaimed prophet of the railways. A few years earlier James had visited George Stephenson's Killingworth shop and was so impressed by the steam locomotives that he agreed to try to sell them for a percentage of the profits.

The Liverpool group hired James, who in turn hired George and Robert Stephenson, to survey the land and draw up plans for a thirty-five-mile (fifty-six-kilometer) railway between Liverpool and Manchester. Stephenson, seeing this as the perfect opportunity to promote his new locomotives, gradually tried to take complete control of the project. He was named chief engineer of the L&MR when James became ill and was unable to complete the plans.

In its time, the L&MR was the greatest challenge of British civil engineering. Several nat-

ural obstacles had to be conquered over the rough terrain between the two cities. First was Chat Moss, an immense thirty-foot- (nine-meter-) deep bog that many skeptics thought could never be crossed. Considered a death trap that could swallow a man whole, Chat Moss proved to be the cheapest and smoothest part of the line. Instead of trying to fill or drain the bog, the resourceful Stephenson instead simply floated his track across it on a continuous raft made of brushwood and heather.

The most difficult part of the line came at the Manchester end, where another bog had to be filled with a thousand tons (907 metric tons) of landfill before it could be crossed. This section proved very expensive in terms of both money and lives.

At the western end of the line stood Olive Mount, where workers had to cut through seventy feet (twenty-one meters) of solid sandstone in order to maintain the proper gradient. As if that weren't enough, a nine-arch viaduct, the longest one built to date, had to be constructed to carry the line over Sankey

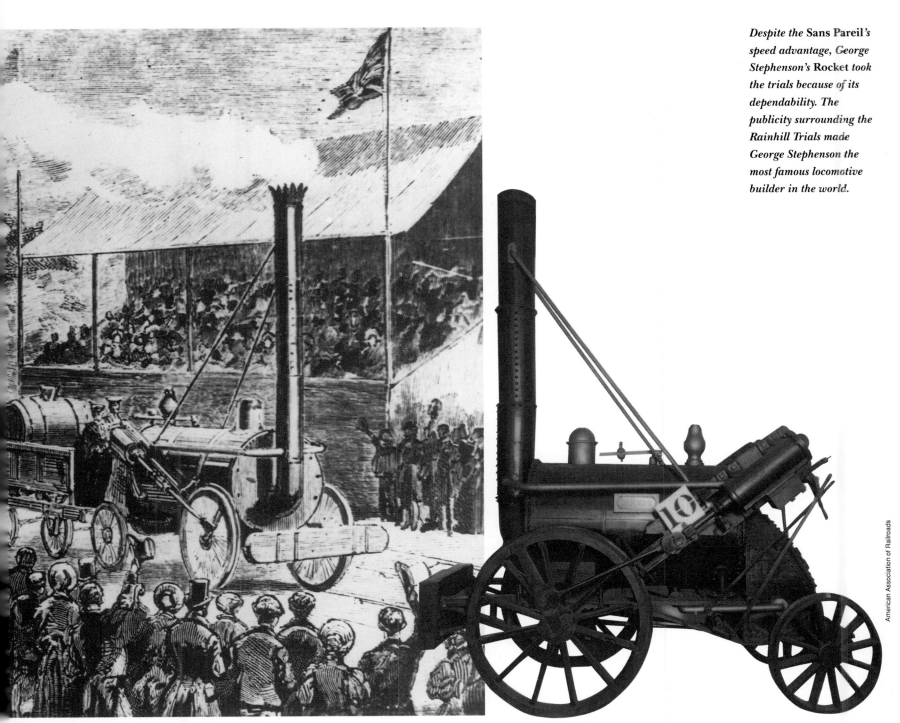

*Despite the **Sans Pareil's** speed advantage, George Stephenson's **Rocket** took the trials because of its dependability. The publicity surrounding the Rainhill Trials made George Stephenson the most famous locomotive builder in the world.*

American Association of Railroads

Valley. Completing the line was a tunnel under Liverpool leading to the docks. All in all the L&MR required a total of sixty-three bridges, viaducts, and tunnels to cover the thirty-five-mile (fifty-six-kilometer) journey.

The Rainhill Trails

As the project neared completion, L&MR directors became wary of the reliability of steam locomotion. Much to the consternation of the Stephensons, a few of the directors pushed for a system of rope haulage and horse-powered carriages. After much negotiation, a compromise was finally reached, and in October 1829, the directors invited locomotive builders to prove the reliability of their machines at a section of track near Liverpool, known as Rainhill. A first prize of £500 was offered to the best 4.5 ton (four metric ton) locomotive that could haul three times its weight for more than seventy miles (one hundred twelve kilometers) without stopping at an average speed of no less than ten miles (sixteen kilometers) per hour.

Three locomotives were entered in the competition: the *Novelty*, built by John Braithwaite and John Ericsson (Ericsson would later go on to revolutionize naval architecture with his iron-clad warship, the *Monitor*); the *Sans Pareil*, built by Timothy Hackworth; and the *Rocket*, built by George and Robert Stephenson. The *Novelty* won the praise of the spectators by reaching a top speed of forty miles (sixty-four kilometers) per hour, as compared to the *Rocket*, which reached twenty-nine miles (forty-six kilometers) per hour and *Sans Pareil*, which reached seventeen miles (twenty-seven kilometers) per hour. The *Novelty* also achieved the greatest fuel economy by burning only a half a pound of coke for each ton of weight moved across a one-mile (1.6-kilometer) distance. The problem with Braithwaite and Ericsson's speedy machine was that it was plagued by breakdowns throughout the competition (as was the slow *Sans Pareil*).

The *Rocket*, on the other hand, rambled through the forty road tests without a hitch. For dependability and practicality, the

*The **Rocket** is still recognized as the main ancestor of the modern steam locomotive. Stephenson incorporated many innovations that would serve the steam locomotive for more than one hundred years.*

Stephensons' locomotive outclassed the competition and put to rest the doubts of even the most skeptical directors. Their innovative *Rocket* was the first locomotive to combine all of the fundamentals that would serve railroad locomotives for more than a century to come: a multitubular boiler, separate twin pistons with direct drive to the wheels, and a crankshaft driving system. Along with the £500 prize, the Stephensons gained a reputation for being the premiere locomotive builders in the world. Now the stage was set for the grand opening of the pioneer L&MR on September 15, 1830. The event was not without political consequences.

The Tories, The Canningites, and The First Railroad Fatality

William Huskisson was the leader of the Progressive Tories, or Canningites, a faction of the Tory party that had sprung up around the late prime minister George Canning. The Canningites broke from the ruling Tory party when Huskisson resigned from the Duke of Wellington's government over its refusal to accept the enfranchisement of Manchester. England was in the middle of a reform crisis and Huskisson knew that the Duke would need the help and support of the Canningites if the government were to have any hope of de-

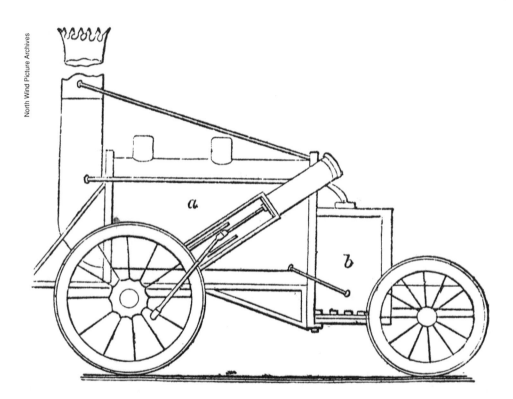

feating the Reform Act and keeping the Whigs and the Radicals from power. Huskisson saw the Manchester enfranchisement, a relatively minor parliamentary reform, as an opportunity to gain power for himself.

In order to negotiate a reconciliation, Huskisson and the Duke staged a chance meeting at the much-publicized grand opening of the L&MR, England's greatest engineering accomplishment. Eight trains would carry more than 1,000 passengers with more than 50,000 spectators cheering them along.

As the inaugural train pulled out of Liverpool's Crown Street Station, the Duke, Huskisson, and several other political leaders and dignitaries rode in a lavish, crimson-canopied coach topped by a dual coronet. Several miles down the track, the train stopped at Parkside to take on water. As Huskisson and a few others got off to stretch their legs and get some air, another of the Stephensons' trains bore down on them on the return track. The group of men scrambled to get back into their canopied car, but Huskisson, who was slightly paralyzed on one side, was not fast enough to get out of the way.

"Huskisson," shouted a panicked Duke, "do get to your place! For God's sake, get to your place!" Huskisson made it as far as the door, with one hand on the latch, when he slipped and fell in the path of the oncoming train. George Stephenson quickly attached the *Northumbrian* to a single car and rushed the fallen politician at breakneck speed back to Eccles. The steam-driven ambulance was not quick enough, however, and Huskisson died along the way.

In November of that same year the Reform Act was passed and the Duke's government was forced to resign; the power in England shifted from the old aristocrats to the new industrial capitalists, who stood the most to gain from the development of steam-powered railways. To what degree this first railroad fatality contributed to the fall of Wellington is a matter of historical speculation, but one thing was certain: Despite the initial mishap, the Liverpool & Manchester Railway was a huge success. By 1831, the L&MR transported more than 1,000 passengers a day and had become the model for other pioneer railroads around the world.

Stephenson's Northumbrian was quickly turned into a makeshift ambulance after Canningite leader William Huskisson was hit by a train in the world's first railroad fatality. Despite the accident, the grand opening of the Liverpool and Manchester Railway was a great success.

The First North American Railways

One of the earliest American proponents of steam-powered locomotion was a New Jersey farmer named Colonel John Stevens. In order to prove the viability of such a project, Stevens set up an experimental railway in 1825 on his farm in Hoboken, New Jersey.

North America was much more resistant to the idea of railways than was England. The majority of industrialists still considered canals the best form of transportation. In spite of them, a few innovative thinkers were convinced that railways, more specifically, steam-powered railways, were the wave of the future.

As early as 1812, a New Jersey farmer named Colonel John Stevens published an article entitled *Documents Tending to Prove the Superior Advantages of Railways and Steam Carriages over Canal Navigation*. In this article Stevens made the then outrageous statement: "I can see nothing to hinder a steam-engine from moving at a velocity of 100 miles an hour. In practice, it may not be advisable to exceed 20 or 30 miles an hour, but I should not be surprised at seeing carriages propelled at 40 or 50."

A friend to some of the most influential men in the Hudson River Valley, Stevens was also highly respected for his mechanical ability and foresight. This, however, was not enough to keep him from being the subject of much ridicule for his outlandish prediction.

Stevens ignored his detractors and, in 1815, gained a charter from the New Jersey government for the laying of track between New Brunswick and Trenton, the first railway charter ever issued in the United States. In 1823,

Pennsylvania granted Stevens a charter for a railway between Philadelphia and the Susquehanna River.

Unable to raise money for either venture, Colonel Stevens built a 630-foot (1008-kilometer) oval track and a small, steam-powered locomotive on his farm in Hoboken, New Jersey, in the hopes of impressing investors. Steven's locomotive was very primitive by British standards: It was powered by a single cylinder and used a cog-wheel arrangement similar to the one used by Matthew Murray in London twelve years earlier. Stevens's tiny locomotive, however, did not impress many investors. It was bad timing: At about the same time Stevens chugged around his small track, five hundred cannons, spread from Buffalo to the Atlantic Ocean, were fired off announcing the grand opening of the Erie Canal.

This unparalleled feat of civil engineering quickly became a huge financial success, spurring a rash of canal planning and building across the United States. The Erie Canal, however, was blessed with ample natural waterways and relatively flat terrain. Builders and surveyors would soon find out that other canal projects would not be quite so easy.

One such project was the Delaware & Hudson Canal, which was to connect the anthracite mines in northeastern Pennsylvania to the Hudson River at Rondout, New York. John Jervis, a former engineer on the Erie Canal, was appointed head of the project. The

Smithsonian Institution

canal progressed smoothly from Rondout until it reached Mt. Moosic in Honesdale, Pennsylvania, sixteen miles (twenty-six kilometers) from its destination. The mountain proved too tall for a practical system of locks, so Jarvis decided to build a railway to cover the final distance. Stationary steam engines with rope haulage were to be used for the steep sections of track followed by horse-powered carriages for the remaining flat sections.

As the laying of track progressed, Jervis became increasingly interested in using steam locomotives similar to those already in wide use in England. After gaining consent from the directors of the canal company, Jervis sent his twenty-six-year-old assistant, Horatio Allen, to England to purchase four locomotives. In the summer of 1829, Allen returned with the *America*, the *Delaware*, the *Hudson*, and the *Stourbridge Lion*. The *Stourbridge Lion* made the initial run on August 8, 1829. Horatio Allen later wrote:

He who addresses you was the only person on that locomotive. The circumstances which led to my being alone on the engine were these: The road had been built in the summer; the structure was of hemlock timber, the rails of large dimensions notched on caps placed far apart. The timber was cracked and warped from exposure to the sun. After 300 feet of straight line, the road crossed the Lackawaxen Creek on a trestle about 30 feet high, and with a curve of 350 to 400 feet radius. The impression was very general

that this iron monster would break down the road, or that it would leave the track at the curve and plunge into the creek. My reply... was that it was too late to consider the probability of such circumstances... that I would take the first ride alone and the time would come when I should look back to the incident with great interest.

As I place my hand upon the throttle valve handle I was undecided whether I should move slowly or with a fair degree of speed. But holding that the road would prove safe, and preferring, if we did go down, to go down handsomely, and without any evidence of timidity, I started with considerable velocity, passed the curves over the creek safely, and was soon out of hearing of the cheering of the vast assemblage present. At the end of two or three miles I reversed the valve, and returned without incident to the place of starting, having made the first locomotive trip in the Western Hemisphere.

As it turned out, the seven-ton (six-metric-ton) *Lion* was too heavy for the fragile track and caused such damage that its use was discontinued. The *Lion* was put in storage at Honesdale along with its three sister locomotives. Many years later the engine was restored and donated to the Smithsonian Institute in Washington, D.C, where it resides today.

American Association of Railroads

In 1829, a young Horatio Allen was sent to England to purchase four locomotives for use on the tracks of the Delaware & Hudson Canal Company in Honesdale, Pennsylvania. Out of the four locomotives, only one, the **Stourbridge Lion** *(top), ever journeyed down the tracks. Horatio would later go on to become the Chief Engineer of the South Carolina Railroad.*

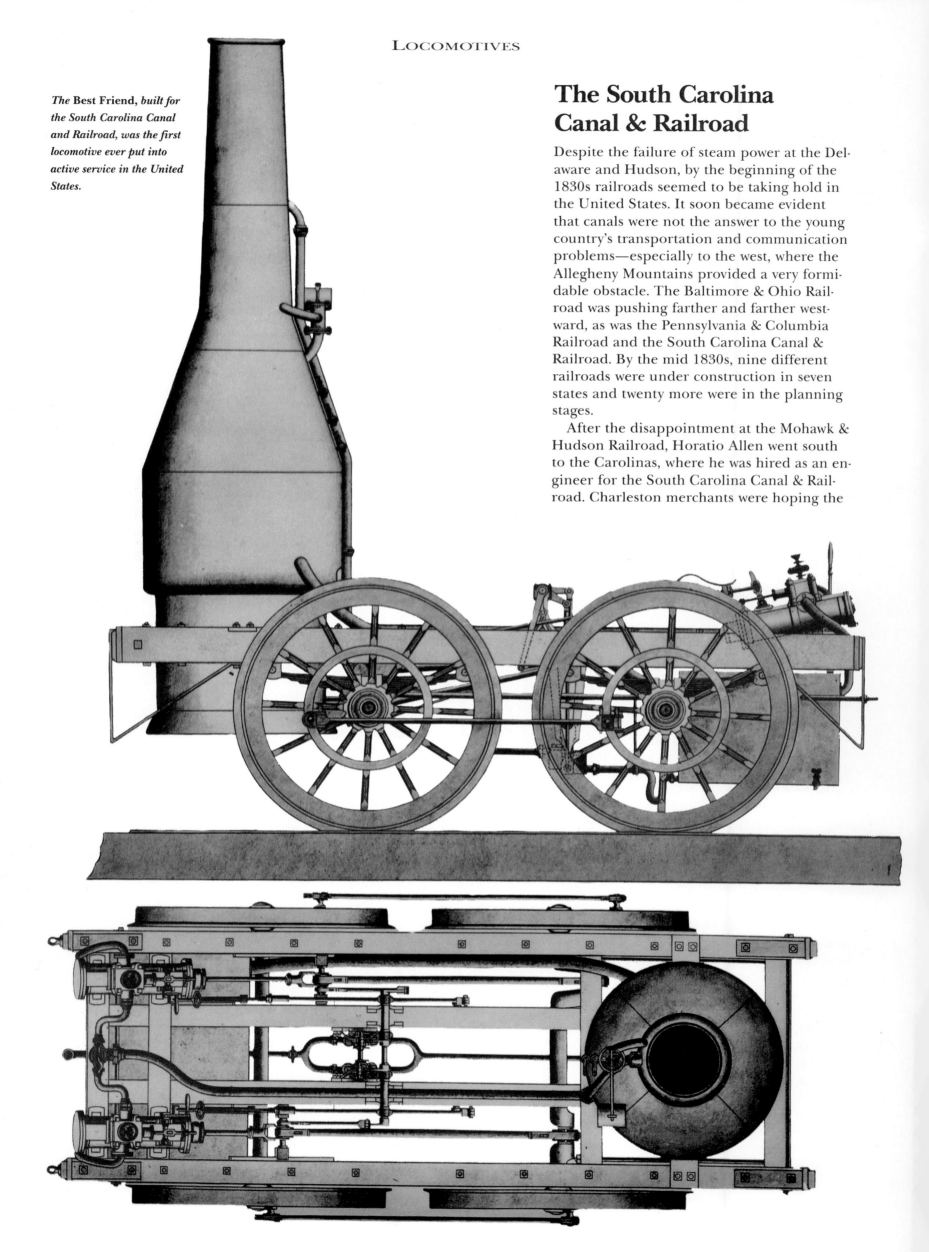

The **Best Friend,** *built for the South Carolina Canal and Railroad, was the first locomotive ever put into active service in the United States.*

The South Carolina Canal & Railroad

Despite the failure of steam power at the Delaware and Hudson, by the beginning of the 1830s railroads seemed to be taking hold in the United States. It soon became evident that canals were not the answer to the young country's transportation and communication problems—especially to the west, where the Allegheny Mountains provided a very formidable obstacle. The Baltimore & Ohio Railroad was pushing farther and farther westward, as was the Pennsylvania & Columbia Railroad and the South Carolina Canal & Railroad. By the mid 1830s, nine different railroads were under construction in seven states and twenty more were in the planning stages.

After the disappointment at the Mohawk & Hudson Railroad, Horatio Allen went south to the Carolinas, where he was hired as an engineer for the South Carolina Canal & Railroad. Charleston merchants were hoping the new canal-railroad combination would help revitalize their faltering economy. Allen convinced the financial backers of the project that a horse-powered tramway would not be efficient enough to help Charleston compete on a national basis. He assured them that the 136-mile (218-kilometer) rail section of the project would be best served by the fast and powerful "iron horse."

With the blessings of the nervous investors, Allen hired two local men to design an engine: E.L. Miller, a prominent Charleston merchant and C.E. Detmold, a mechanic and inventor. Actual construction of the engine was completed in New York City during the summer of 1830 by the West Point Foundry, a manufacturer of ship fittings. The result was a five-ton (four-metric-ton) engine aptly named *Best Friend of Charleston*.

On a brisk Christmas Day in 1830, *Best Friend* made its auspicious first run, pulling a series of cars carrying 200 of Charleston's most elite socialites. The train completed the six-mile (ten-kilometer) run without a mishap, becoming the first successful commercial locomotive built in the Western Hemisphere.

A year and a half later, however, the *Best Friend* was to meet a most unfortunate demise. In June 1831, it was making an early morning freight run when the safety valve started screaming because of the excessive heat of the engine's fire. The unthinking fireman tied down the safety valve to stop the annoying hiss. Pressure built up in the boiler, and the *Best Friend* soon blew its top with a deafening roar.

Miraculously, an engineer named Julius Petsh gathered up the scattered pieces and managed to salvage the nearly disintegrated engine. The rebuilt engine was appropriately named the *Phoenix*, after the mythological bird that rose from the flames of its own funeral pyre. In order to reassure worried passengers, the railroad company announced that all future trains would include a barrier car loaded with six bales of cotton between the engine and the passengers. According to an advertisement, the barrier car would "protect travelers when the locomotive explodes."

The Baltimore & Ohio Railroad

About the same time as the *Best Friend of Charleston* was making its initial runs on the South Carolina Canal & Railroad, the Baltimore & Ohio Railroad directors were faced with the difficult decision of what form of traction to use, horse or steam. The B&O was the longest and most complicated railroad ever built in the United States, and it was to provide an invaluable link to the Northwest Territory. To help them with their choice, the directors of the B&O asked the advice of the venerable George Stephenson of England. The uncharacteristically discouraging Stephenson advised against steam power for the B&O, stating that it possessed curves that were too tight for a steam locomotive to negotiate. Stephenson maintained that a steam engine required a turning radius of no less than 900 feet (274 meters). Because of rough terrain, the B&O was built with turns as tight as 400 feet (121 meters).

In 1829, Peter Cooper built the Tom Thumb, the first locomotive to be built in the United States. This diminutive locomotive was created solely to impress the directors of the Baltimore & Ohio Railroad, and was never used for active service.

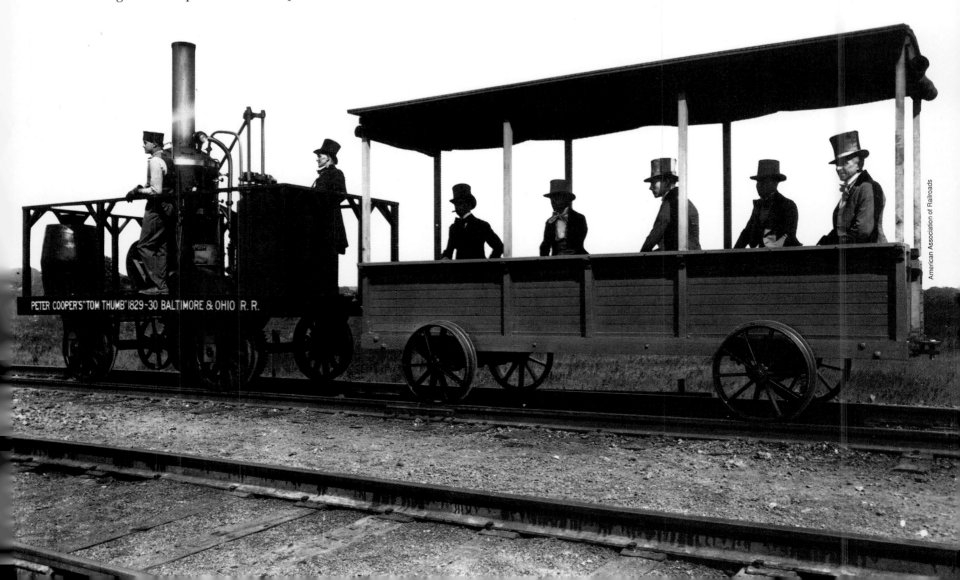

PETER COOPER'S "TOM THUMB" 1829~30 BALTIMORE & OHIO R. R.

American Association of Railroads

The Mount Clare Station is the first and oldest passenger station in the world. On August 25, 1835, the first train to enter Washington, D.C. left from this station.

The B&O directors seemed set on settling for traditional horse cars when they were visited by New York philanthropist Peter Cooper. Concerned that several of his investments would suffer if the new railroad was not a success, Cooper was intent on convincing the directors that steam power was the better choice. Cooper knew that if the B&O chose horse power, it could not hope to compete with the nearly completed Potomac Canal.

Cooper took Stephenson's discouragement as a personal challenge. He went back to New York and built a steam engine of his own. Throwing together odds and ends of sheet metal and boiler iron, even using two broken musket barrels for tubes in his boiler (no metal tubes were being made in America at the time), Cooper built a small one-ton (.9-metric-ton) engine called the *Tom Thumb* "because it was so insignificant. I didn't intend it for actual service, but only to show the directors that it could be done."

Cooper brought the machine to Baltimore, where he attached it to a wagon full of investors and pulled them along a thirteen-mile (twenty-one-kilometer) section of track ending at Ellicotts Mills. Reaching a top speed of twenty miles (thirty-two kilometers) per hour, the small machine negotiated the tight curves with relative ease. On its return trip, *Tom Thumb* met up with a horse-drawn wagon where a section of double track began. An impromptu race naturally ensued. *Tom Thumb* outsped the filly most of the way, but relinquished the lead when it literally ran out of

steam. While Cooper's machine lost the race, it did impress the B&O directors enough for them to announce their own version of the Rainhill Trials for American-made locomotives.

A first prize of $4,000 was offered to the best four-wheeled locomotive weighing no more than 3.5 tons (three metric tons), capable of hauling fifteen tons (fourteen metric tons) at an average speed of fifteen miles (twenty-four kilometers) per hour on level track. Five locomotives entered the trials; the prize ultimately went to the *York*, built by a Pennsylvania watchmaker named Phineas Davis. Since the *York* was not ready for practical use on the B&O, Davis was given the chance to go back to the shop and design a much larger, seven-ton (six-metric-ton) machine capable of heavy freight and passenger haulage. A year later Davis returned with the *Atlantic*, a huge engine that conformed to the B&O's strict limitations of clearance and turning radius.

In 1833, a tragic accident led to the death of the *Atlantic*'s determined creator. An excerpt of a B&O's board of director's meeting reads: "On September 27, [Phineas Davis] having completed a new engine, availed himself of the occasion of trying it to take his numerous workmen on a visit to Washington. On his return the engine, striking the end of a rail, which the breaking of an iron chair had permitted to get out of alignment, was thrown from the structure, and, being on the tender, he was dashed forward against the engine and instantly killed."

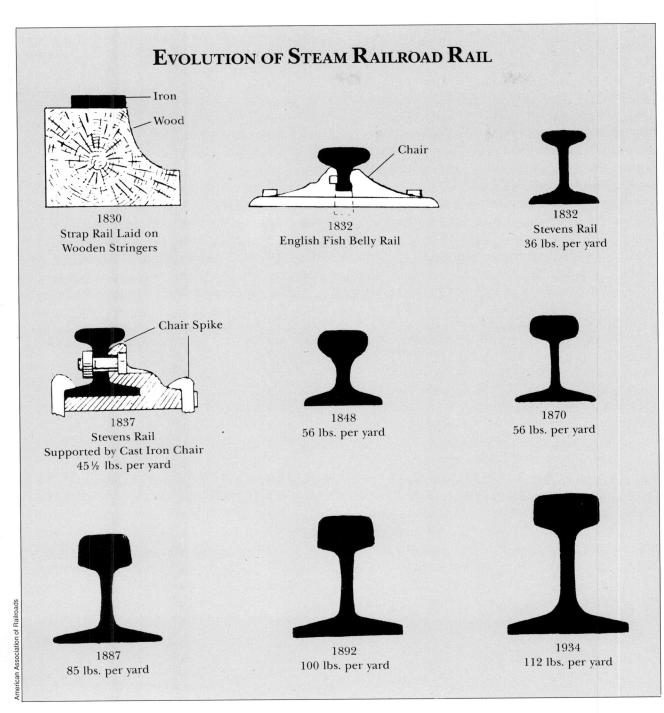

EVOLUTION OF STEAM RAILROAD RAIL

Iron
Wood

1830
Strap Rail Laid on
Wooden Stringers

Chair

1832
English Fish Belly Rail

1832
Stevens Rail
36 lbs. per yard

Chair Spike

1837
Stevens Rail
Supported by Cast Iron Chair
45½ lbs. per yard

1848
56 lbs. per yard

1870
56 lbs. per yard

1887
85 lbs. per yard

1892
100 lbs. per yard

1934
112 lbs. per yard

American Association of Railroads

On October 13, 1830, Robert Stevens (Colonel John Steven's son) set sail for England with the purpose of buying a locomotive and a load of track. While en route he carved what would become the standard track design out of a block of wood. This basic design has lasted for years with few changes.

The Camden & Amboy Railroad

In 1830, the New Jersey Legislature approved a charter for a railroad between Raritan Bay and the Delaware River community of Bordentown, following the original route proposed by Colonel John Stevens fifteen years earlier. This time, however, the project had no trouble attracting investors: $4 million worth of stock was sold in exactly ten minutes. Colonel Stevens's son, Robert, was put in charge of the project. Twenty-one years earlier, Robert Stevens had gained fame by captaining the first open-sea voyage of a steamboat—a thirteen-day trip from Hoboken, New Jersey, around Cape May, New Jersey, to Philadelphia, Pennsylvania, made in one of his father's steamboats.

On October 13, 1830, the younger Stevens set sail for England with the purpose of buying a locomotive and a load of iron track. Stevens felt that the British "fish-belly" track set on iron chairs was too expensive and too complicated for eventual production by American foundries. So with a jackknife and a block of pine in hand, Stevens whittled out a new track design. The result was the inverted T-rail that is still in use today. The new track could be easily fastened with an offset-headed spike. Once in England he found a Welsh foundryman to roll the unusual track. While the rails were being made, Stevens met with George Stephenson and bought one of his Sampson-type engines.

Stevens arrived in Philadelphia with twenty-two crates of sixteen-foot (five-meter) rails and a disassembled engine. The entire cargo was then shipped up the Delaware to Bordentown. Faced with a mass of unlabeled parts and no Stephenson mechanic to aid in assembly, Stevens hired a twenty-two-year-old shipwright's apprentice named Isaac Dripps to figure out the locomotive puzzle. Stevens and Dripps worked together in fitting together Stephenson's machine, adding a few parts of their own when needed. The result was a hybrid locomotive originally called the *Stevens*, later renamed the *John Bull*. Their new engine included four innovations that served railroading for many years.

Robert Stevens returned from England with a disassembled Stephenson locomotive. As he and shipwright's apprentice Isaac Dripps attempted to put the complicated locomotive together, they made several changes to Stephenson's design. The result was a hybrid locomotive named the **John Bull.**

First, Dripps added bogie wheels to a forward extension on the train. This helped distribute the weight of the engine as well as guide the train through sharp turns. On top of this extension, Dripps added what would become the first effective cow catcher. The scooplike device pushed aside any stray animals that may have wandered onto the track. The Pennsylvania & Reading Railroad had already installed their own type of cow catcher, but their two-pronged device tended to skewer the cattle instead of pushing them aside.

One of the major improvements of the *John Bull* was the trumpet-shaped stack, which redirected hot embers back into the fire. This fire stack was eventually adapted into the balloon, sunflower, and cabbage-head stacks, all of which were used well into the twentieth century. Finally, Dripps added a fuel truck directly behind the engine along with a "gig-top" cube to help protect the engine crew from smoke and embers.

The track for the Camden & Amboy line was laid using stone blocks with maple dowels in the center. The rails were laid on the blocks and spikes were driven into the dowels to secure the track. Stevens had arranged for prisoners at Sing Sing to make the stone bases, but as the railroad reached South Amboy, New Jersey, production from Sing Sing slowed, delaying completion of the line. In order to meet construction deadlines, the resourceful Stevens completed the track using wooden cross ties. Initially a temporary measure, the wooden cross ties worked better than the stone bases, and Stevens eventually replaced the rest of the stone with wood.

On November 12, 1831, the *John Bull* carried its first passengers down the Camden & Amboy Railroad. Among the riders were Joseph Bonaparte, Napoleon's eldest brother, who was by this time a Delaware farmer, having failed as King of Naples and King of Spain; and Napoleon's niece, Madam Marat, one of the first women to ride on a train.

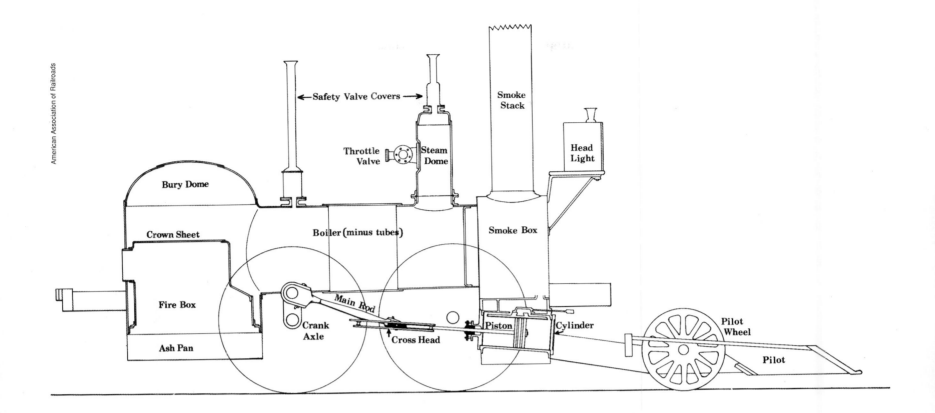

Safety Valve Covers

Smoke Stack

Throttle Valve

Steam Dome

Head Light

Bury Dome

Boiler (minus tubes)

Smoke Box

Crown Sheet

Fire Box

Main Rod

Crank Axle

Piston

Cylinder

Pilot Wheel

Cross Head

Pilot

Ash Pan

Not everyone greeted the new railroads with open arms, as can be seen in this tract protesting the building of the Camden and Amboy Railroad. *Old Ironsides,* the first locomotive built by Matthias W. Baldwin, made its inaugural run on November 23, 1832 on the Philadelphia, Germantown, and Norristown Railroad.

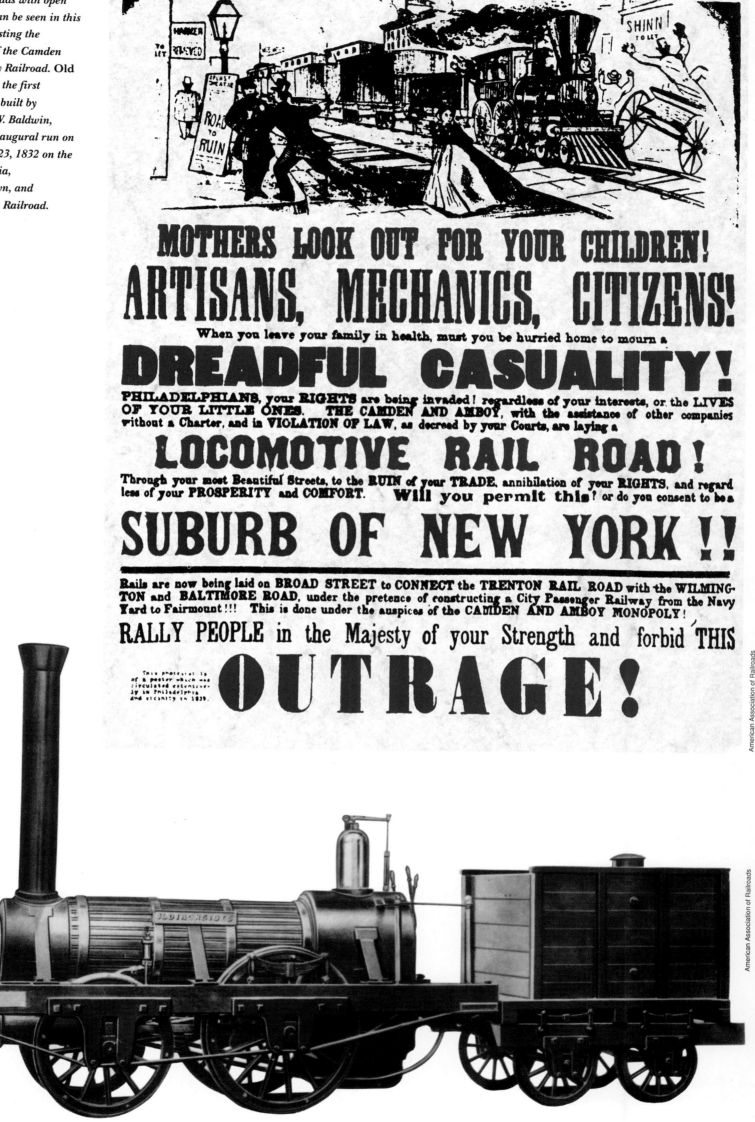

MOTHERS LOOK OUT FOR YOUR CHILDREN!
ARTISANS, MECHANICS, CITIZENS!
When you leave your family in health, must you be hurried home to mourn a
DREADFUL CASUALITY!
PHILADELPHIANS, your RIGHTS are being invaded! regardless of your interests, or the LIVES OF YOUR LITTLE ONES. THE CAMDEN AND AMBOY, with the assistance of other companies without a Charter, and in VIOLATION OF LAW, as decreed by your Courts, are laying a
LOCOMOTIVE RAIL ROAD!
Through your most Beautiful Streets, to the RUIN of your TRADE, annihilation of your RIGHTS, and regard less of your PROSPERITY and COMFORT. Will you permit this? or do you consent to be a
SUBURB OF NEW YORK!!
Rails are now being laid on BROAD STREET to CONNECT the TRENTON RAIL ROAD with the WILMINGTON and BALTIMORE ROAD, under the pretence of constructing a City Passenger Railway from the Navy Yard to Fairmount!!! This is done under the auspices of the CAMDEN AND AMBOY MONOPOLY!
RALLY PEOPLE in the Majesty of your Strength and forbid THIS
OUTRAGE!

This photostat is of a poster which was circulated extensively in Philadelphia and vicinity in 1839.

The Baldwin Locomotive Works

Later in 1831, a former watchmaker from Philadelphia, Pennsylvania, Matthias W. Baldwin, went to Bordentown to inspect the *John Bull*. Baldwin had been commissioned by the Philadelphia, Germantown, & Norristown Railroad to build an engine based on the Stephenson design.

A few years earlier, Baldwin had abandoned the watchmaking business to become a manufacturer of bookbinding tools. In the course of his business he designed a very compact and reliable steam engine to drive his lathes. Word of his machine spread and Baldwin was soon inundated with orders for similar steam engines.

One of the more unusual orders came from Benjamin Franklyn Peale, son of noted artist, scientist, and politician Charles Wilson Peale. The younger Peale managed a local museum that specialized in natural history and mechanical wonders. He wanted to install an interactive exhibit that consisted of a small steam engine and a track inside the museum to transport people around. Peale began installing the track and asked Baldwin to design the engine. Working from newspaper reports of the Rainhill Trials, Baldwin designed a small engine. It drew huge crowds after its installation in the museum on April 25, 1831. Among the people who first rode on the indoor train were the directors of the Philadelphia, Germantown, & Norristown Railroad, who eventually offered Baldwin $4,000 to duplicate a Stephenson machine. Despite the low pay—materials alone would cost more than $4,000—Baldwin jumped at the chance to work on a full-scale locomotive.

Baldwin had problems finding foundries able to do the necessary work, yet still managed to build *Old Ironsides* in a little over a year. The five-ton (four-metric-ton) locomotive made its first six-mile (ten-kilometer) run on November 23, 1832. From his original success with *Old Ironsides*, Baldwin went on to build the *W.L Miller* for the South Carolina Railroad and the *Lancaster* and the *Neversink* for the Philadelphia & Reading Railroad. By 1837, the railroad boom was in full swing: Tracks were being laid across the country and orders for Baldwin locomotives were pouring in. Over the next 118 years the Baldwin Locomotive Works produced 80,000 steam engines, more than any other locomotive manufacturer in the world.

Despite many irrational fears of railroad travel (people thought the high speeds of steam locomotives would cause permanent brain damage and that just watching a speeding train could drive a person mad), the steam locomotive had become an established part of American transportation plans by the early 1830s. This fact was made even more evident when Andrew Jackson became the first United States president to ride a train; he took a trip on the Baltimore & Ohio (the Queen of England would not take her first ride for seven more years). The age of the railroad was at hand.

A former watchmaker and bookbinder from Philadelphia, Matthias W. Baldwin went on to create the largest locomotive works in the world. In 118 years of operation, the Baldwin Locomotive Works built over 80,000 steam locomotives.

CHAPTER THREE

THE RAILROAD BOOM

ONLY FIFTY YEARS AFTER THE OPENING OF THE first successful public railway, steam locomotives were the primary form of transportation in both Europe and the United States. By 1850, the United States had 9,000 route miles (14,400 kilometers) of track. Ten years later, the number shot up to 30,000 route miles (48,000 kilometers). Because of the railroads, Chicago grew from a town with 29,000 inhabitants to a city with 109,000 in the same ten-year span. The United States rail system reached its zenith in 1916, when more than 250,000 miles (400,000 kilometers) of track were in use.

At the same time, rails were being laid across most of Great Britain and the European continent. By 1913, France had around 25,000 route miles (40,000 kilometers), Germany 18,000 (28,800 kilometers), and Great Britain 15,000 (24,000 kilometers). Travel and trade soon knew no boundaries. The railroad boom between 1850 and 1914 had a drastic effect on the economic and social life of virtually every citizen of every country in the Western world.

North America

In the latter half of the 1800s the United States was expanding geographically and economically. Go west, young man! was the call, and nothing contributed more to westward expansion than the railroads. For every mile of track laid to the west, hundreds of settlers found it easier and more affordable to emigrate. With the opening up of the western

territories came new markets for eastern goods, as well as new supplies of raw materials and food.

The initial westward railroads were designed to link the east with the midwest's natural waterways—the Great Lakes, the Ohio River, the Mississippi River, and the Missouri River. These waterways, primarily the large river systems, were the country's north-south highways. With only a few east-west rail lines,

virtually the entire "settled" country at that time could be covered in a huge rail and water transportation grid. At the cornerstone of this potential transportation network was Chicago, the windy city on the lake.

Blessed with excellent water transportation in Lake Michigan as well as a relatively good system of highways, Chicago did not become interested in railroads until the late 1840s. At that time, real estate broker William Butler

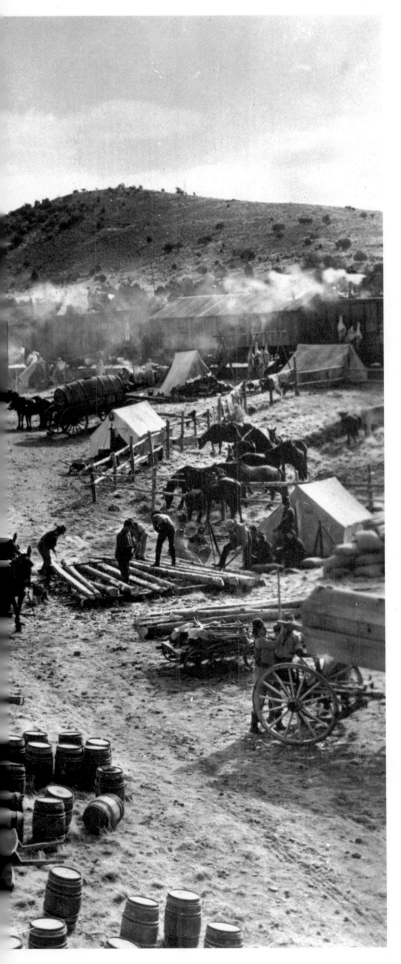

Ogden (who later became the first mayor of Chicago) came up with a plan that would link Chicago with the midwestern prairie lands by means of a steam-operated railroad. The Galena & Chicago Railroad, opened in October 1848, linked the midwest prairie lands to Chicago and the East. Products from the midwest were now available to the entire United States without the high transportation costs of horse-drawn wagons. In addition, this new railroad encouraged the growth of commercial farming in the midwest. Heavy farm machinery could now be shipped from the eastern states to the Mississippi Valley, which then could produce surplus grain to be sold all over the country. Within ten years of its beginning, the fledgling Galena & Chicago Railroad exploded into the powerful Chicago & Northwestern Railroad.

By the 1850s, the first north-south trunk lines were being built, the most important of which was the Illinois Central. Covering 705 miles (1,128 kilometers), from Chicago to the southernmost tip of Illinois at Cairo, the Illinois Central was the longest and costliest mainline in the world. It was also the first railroad in the United States made possible by a land grant. In the late 1840s, the United States government was having trouble selling off land west of Ohio. There simply weren't adequate transportation and communication systems to make the frontier lands desirable to settlers. In 1847, Senator Stephen A. Douglas introduced a bill that granted land to state governments for the purpose of building a state-owned transportation system. The bill eventually passed in 1850, but the provision of state ownership was deleted.

Illinois gave its two-million-acre (81,000 hectare) grant to the Illinois Central Company, which in turn mortgaged most of it off at ten times the price the United States government had been able to sell it at. All in all, the Illinois Central Company made $17 million—more than enough to start their ambitious railroad project. In subsequent years, more than twenty million acres (810,000 hectares) of land was granted for building railroads in the midwest, and after the Civil War, handouts were even greater—more than 300,000 square miles (777,000 square kilometers) in all were granted for railroad building.

By 1860, Chicago was the hub of eleven different railroads that reached as far west as Missouri and as far south as Louisiana. Between 1850 and 1861 the total railroad miles in the United States jumped from 10,000 to 30,000 (16,000 to 48,000 kilometers). As the railroad boom intensified, its center of concentration shifted from the industrial east to the agricultural midwest. The country was rapidly growing; new territories were opening up and new states were being formed. But along with this rapid expansion came domestic unrest. By 1861, the Confederacy seceded and the Civil War broke out.

As the United States expanded westward, so too did the railroads. In the eleven years between 1850 and 1861 alone, the number of active railroad miles in the United States jumped from 10,000 to 30,000 miles (16,000 to 48,000 km).

American Association of Railroads

The Civil War and The Railroads

The United States Civil War was the first war in which the railroad played a significant role: It was used for supplying men, food, and ammunition to the warring armies. Unfortunately for the Confederacy, the North had a better planned and equipped railroad system. It contained three times as many rail miles and five times as many locomotives as the South. More importantly, the North's vast east-west connections made western and midwestern resources readily available.

The railroads in both the North and the South took a tremendous beating during the Civil War. Because of their tremendous strategic importance, they were frequent targets of attack. Track was ripped up, engines were destroyed, and bridges were burned. During their march through the South, General Sherman's army ripped up over 500 miles (800 kilometers) of track and gutted more than fifty engines.

Despite all of this damage, the railroad companies still managed to make a lot of money during the Civil War. The railroads were busier during the war than at any other time in their history, and the railroad barons were unscrupulous. They would run barricades to deliver food and supplies to whoever could pay for them—the Confederate Louisville & Nashville Railroad made a great deal of money by servicing both the North and the South.

Perhaps the best-known Civil War story involving the railroads was that of *The General*, made famous in a film by Buster Keaton. *The General* was a Confederate 4-4-0 locomotive hijacked by Captain James Andrews and a band of scouts near Chattanooga, Tennessee in 1862. Andrews's intention was to run north with *The General*, tearing up track and destroying bridges along the way, thereby cutting Confederate supply lines. However, a band of resourceful Confederate railroad men took chase in a locomotive called the *Texas*. The Union soldiers on *The General* tried everything to stop the tireless chase of the *Texas*. They tried destroying sections of track. They sent a wagon crashing back down the track to run into the oncoming train. They even set a bridge on fire, but none of these obstacles could stop the hard-charging Confederates. The *Texas* pursued, until its last lump of coal and stick of wood was burned. While it never did catch *The General*, the *Texas* did manage to keep the railroad operational and Confederate supply lines open.

The railroads played a major role in supplying men, food, and ammunition during the Civil War. With thousands of more rail miles and hundreds of more locomotives, the industrialized North had a distinct advantage over the chiefly agricultural South.

North Wind Picture Archives

The Transcontinental Railroad

After a brief delay from 1861 into the beginning of 1862 railroad building began again in earnest when President Lincoln signed a Bill authorizing land grants and loans for the purpose of building a transcontinental railroad. At a time when the country was split, the symbolism of linking the east coast with the west coast by means of an iron rail could not be missed. One of the main reasons the South seceded in the first place was over the issue of whether or not the new western states would be slave states. By authorizing a transcontinental railroad at this time, Lincoln established a strong foothold in the west.

According to the plan, the Union Pacific was to run a line east from Sacramento, California. Meanwhile, the Central Pacific would run a line west from Omaha, Missouri, and the two lines would meet somewhere in the vicinity of Nevada or Utah. Construction on the two lines officially began in 1863. In the first few years of construction the Central Pacific laid down track efficiently and methodically, running into few major problems.

North Wind Picture Archives

At a time when a very young United States was being torn apart by civil war, President Lincoln proposed joining the two coasts with a steel rail. This was the most ambitious rail project ever attempted. The work force, which jumped from 250 men in 1865 to more than 10,000 by the railroad's completion, was made up mostly of Irish, Chinese, and European immigrants. Their average pay was $3 a day.

Meanwhile, the Union Pacific, plagued by management problems, inexperience, and rough terrain, laid an abysmal forty miles (sixty-four kilometers) of track in the first two years. At that rate, the Central Pacific would have been in the Union Pacific's territory long before the specified deadline.

In 1866 Union Pacific's management hired the Casement brothers, a contracting duo from Ohio with an impeccable reputation for being able to get any job done. The Casements reorganized the entire Union Pacific Company and its work force. The two brothers inspired their workers by turning the entire project into a race with the haughty Central Pacific. Despite the problems of warring Native Americans, the Union Pacific managed to triple its output in less than a year. As the project neared completion, the Union Pacific workers laid nearly eight miles (thirteen kilometers) of track in a single day. Company vice president T.C. Durant was so impressed by this accomplishment that he bet the Central Pacific $10,000 they could not better it. Only two days before the ends met, the Central Pacific shattered the Union Pacific's record by laying more than ten miles (sixteen kilometers) of track in one day.

The continent was linked when a single gold spike was driven into the ground connecting the two railroads at Promontory Point, Utah on May 10, 1869. Over 1,750 miles (2,800 kilometers) of track had been laid by the two companies in only four years, and, for the first time, coast-to-coast rail travel was possible in the United States.

Along with the possibility of transcontinental travel came an unforeseen problem. Un-

like the more advanced British rail system, the United States railroads lacked a unified system of signalling and switching. Although telegraph lines were run along the tracks, trains still worked on a system of elaborate timetables. A train would often have to sit for hours at a switching post, waiting for a delayed train to pass in the other direction. The system was made even more complicated by a lack of any standardized time zones. Each community would set their clock according to when the sun rose and set. On a typical transcontinental run a train would pass through more than sixty different time zones. Eventu-

On May 10, 1869, a gold spike was driven in at Promontory, Utah, marking the completion of the first transcontinental. This celebration was attended mostly by politicians, railroad officials, and journalists, while the workers held a separate final spike ceremony (with a steel spike) a few miles down the track (following page).

53

While the original transcontinental railroad is no longer in service, interested tourists can visit the site of this historic union at the Golden Spike National Historic Site outside Promontory, Utah.

ally the railroad companies developed the now familiar eastern, central, mountain, and pacific time zones. This four-zone system was eventually made into law in 1883, despite the objection of many people who felt the railroad barons already had too much control over their lives.

Over the next thirty years, four other transcontinentals were completed: the Northern Pacific (Minnesota to Seattle, 1883); the Great Northern (Minnesota to Seattle, 1893); the Southern Pacific (Los Angeles to New Orleans, 1896); and the Santa Fe (two branches: Chicago to the Gulf of Mexico and Chicago to San Francisco, 1899). By the year 1900, virtually the entire United States was accessible by rail, and for the first time a truly national economy was possible in America.

Cast in 1869 by the William T. Garrett Foundry, the gold spike bears an inscription that reads, "May God continue the unity of our Country, as this Railroad unites the two great Oceans of the world." The spike was later donated to the Stanford University Museum of Art.

Commodore Cornelius Vanderbilt was one of the most notorious of all of the railroad barons. Vanderbilt bought the then small New York Central Railroad and quickly transformed it into a railroad empire with more than 10,000 miles (16,000 km) of track.

Vanderbilt's archenemy was an equally culpable businessman by the name of Daniel Drew. A seasoned stock manipulator, Drew bought his way onto the board of directors of the troubled Erie railroad. Through his position as treasurer, Drew essentially took over the railroad, and reaped millions of dollars.

North Wind Picture Archives

The Railroad Barons

Along with rapid railroad expansion in the United States during the latter part of the nineteenth century came an unprecedented period of greed and corruption among the so-called railroad barons. Vast fortunes were available for the taking, and a few opportunistic individuals stopped at nothing in their endless quest for power.

A prominent railroad baron was Commodore Cornelius Vanderbilt. After already accumulating a multimillion-dollar fortune from his steamboat operations on the Hudson River, Commodore Vanderbilt saw the railroads as a prime opportunity to expand his sphere of influence and his pocketbook. When he was sixty-eight, Vanderbilt bought controlling interest in the then small New York Central Railroad. Through questionable investment practices and land-grabbing schemes, Vanderbilt transformed the New York Central from a small state-based system into a railroad empire that encompassed more than 10,000 rail miles (16,000 kilome-

ters), from Boston, Massachusetts, and New York, New York, as far west as Chicago, Illinois, and St. Louis, Missouri. When some of his associates pointed out that his tactics were not always legal, Vanderbilt was reported to have said, "Law! What do I care about law? Hain't I got the power?"

Between the years 1867 and 1868, the Commodore fell victim to another railroad baron, Daniel Drew, in the much publicized Drew-Vanderbilt War.

When he died in 1877 Vanderbilt passed a fortune of over $100 million along to his son, William Vanderbilt, who had also inherited some of his father's business savvy.

Another veteran of the steamboat business, Drew left naval shipping to amass a larger fortune playing the New York Stock Exchange. From there he bought his way onto the board of directors of the financially troubled Erie Railroad. In 1856, the railroad fell into even worse financial trouble and was in need of immediate cash. Drew came up with a plan where he would lend the railroad the money in exchange for a mortgage on the company's

Drew hired James Fisk (left) and Jay Gould (right) to assist him with the financial misdealings of the Erie Railroad. Through complex financial manipulations on the New York Stock Exchange, the three made themselves rich, while not improving the financial situation of the railroad itself.

small fortune. After losing the financial battle, the Commodore was quoted as saying, "It never pays to kick a skunk."

Drew, however, ended up a victim of his own dirty tactics, when Gould wrested control of the railroad away from him in 1872. Later the same year, Fisk fell victim to a bullet in a quarrel over his mistress.

By this time the Erie was a ruined railroad, so Gould moved out west where he bought controlling interests in the Union Pacific. By paying extraordinarily high dividends, Gould managed to inflate the price of Union Pacific Stock before selling out his shares at a huge profit. He then used his money to buy a series of competing rail routes and began a rate war with the Union Pacific. After Gould

equipment as well as appointment as company treasurer. From this post, he controlled the entire operation. Although he never became president, Drew had the power to determine how and when the company would pay back his loan, and as long as the loan stood, Drew essentially owned the railroad.

In 1864, Drew teamed up with James Fisk and Jay Gould, two accomplished stock manipulators. Through financial wheeling and dealing with Erie stock on the New York Stock Exchange, the three managed to make themselves a fortune without actually improving the value of the railroad itself. One of their victims was the usually indomitable Commodore Vanderbilt. Through a tangle of stock juggling, trickery, malicious and corrupt court actions, and payoffs to the legislature, the trio managed to fleece Vanderbilt out of a

threatened to encroach further in their territory, Union Pacific was forced to buy him off by means of a merger. This resulted in an even larger profit for the unscrupulous Gould. The last of the railroad tycoons, Gould died in 1892, leaving millions of dollars to charity.

Railroad workers formed their first unions during the mid-1860s as a response to the seemingly unbridled power of the railroad tycoons. Unions had little effect on railroad practices until 1877, when the large companies attempted to cut wages. A strike led by the Baltimore & Ohio railroad workers spread through the east and the midwest. Riots ensued as Federal troops were sent in to protect railroad property. It is estimated that as many as 200 people were killed and more than 500 injured before the strike was brought to a bloody end, forever polarizing the now solidified unions and the controlling companies.

Towards the end of the century, government intervention to control the practices of the railroad companies was inevitable. Disgruntled midwestern farmers set up a series of Granger Laws (named after the Grangers, or the Patrons of Husbandry, an association of farmers founded in 1867), which eventually made their way to the Supreme Court in 1886. One year later, the Interstate Commerce Commission (ICC) was formed to control passenger and freight fares. The days of spiraling profits from the railroads were coming to an end. By the 1920s, ICC regulations became so stiff and their control so total that railroad profitability began to dwindle. In essence, the railroad commission intended to save railroads from unscrupulous practices eventually led to its demise.

In the mid 1860s, railroad workers formed their first labor unions to combat low wages and poor working conditions. A strike by the B&O Railroad, however, ended in the death of more than 200 workers.

Howard Mellowes/Envision

Howard Mellowes/Envision

Great Britain

In the early days of the British railway, canals were still the primary mode of freight transport in Great Britain. Trains were used primarily for passenger service and could not compete with the lower freight fares of the canals. By 1867 all of that had changed. The major trunk lines in Great Britain were quite profitable from the huge passenger service market. With that strong financial base, the railroad companies were able to lower their freight costs in order to compete with the canal companies. The lower prices combined with higher speeds and greater efficiency were the undoing of the canal companies. According to the Royal Commission on Railways of 1867:

> In considering the improvement of goods traffic, it is very difficult to institute any comparison with the past, because the introduction of the railway system has entirely altered all the conditions of that traffic, and has enabled industry and trade to spring up which, without railways, could not have existed.

While British railways remained in the hands of private companies, during the 1840s some government intervention became necessary after a proliferation of accidents. This intervention was primarily in the form of inspections and safety regulations. Parliament passed the Railway Regulation Act of 1840 and the Gladstone's Act of 1844. The Railway Department, which was formed as a result of these two acts, was responsible for better riding conditions, improved safety devices and switches, and better working conditions for the railmen.

The rail system had a great social and economic effect on Great Britain. Workers could now travel easily from area to area looking for work, helping to feed the great labor appetite of the Industrial Revolution. Goods were shipped to the most remote corners of the country, and communications were at an all-time high, as a rail-aided British Postal Service could ensure quick delivery of virtually any letter. In addition, the railways and the Industrial Revolution concentrated the majority of the population in towns and cities. By 1851, more people in Britain lived in cities than in the country.

The railway's growth in Britain was phenomenal. By 1851, the railways were carrying 80 million passengers a year, by 1881 over 600 million, by 1901 over 1,100 million. In addition, the average speed of a passenger locomotive went from twelve miles per hour (nineteen kilometers per hour) in 1844 to more than fifty miles per hour (eighty kilometers per hour) by the beginning of the twentieth century.

Throughout the nineteenth century, the British were by far the leaders in railroad development. New locomotive technologies and better tracks increased the speed of the average passenger train from twelve miles (19 km) per hour in 1844 to more than fifty miles (80 km) per hour in 1900.

The Battle of The Gauges

The British rail system was the most advanced in the world; and the best of the British trunk lines was the Great Western Railway (GWR), engineered by Isambard Kingdom Brunel. An unpredictable engineering genius, Brunel possessed a penchant for high-speed rail service. As a result, he designed the GWR with impeccably even grades and few, if any, tight turning radii.

In addition, Brunel, with the aid of his chief engineer Daniel Gooch, adopted a broad track gauge (the distance between the two rails) of 7 feet ¼ inch (2 meters) as opposed to George Stephenson's standard of 4 feet 8 inches (one meter). Brunel maintained that the wider gauge would mean more stability and higher speeds. Of course, Brunel was right. The GWR became the fastest railroad in the world, averaging speeds of sixty miles

per hour (ninety-six kilometers per hour) at certain sections.

The problem came when the GWR had to hook up with neighboring railways. Long delays and sometimes loss of goods occurred as trains had to be switched to the narrower gauge. The train cars would be pulled onto a dual section of track. They would then be unbolted from their chassis and lifted with a crane. A smaller-gauge chassis would be put on the tracks, and the cars would be lowered and bolted to it. Passengers and freight customers alike soon became infuriated by this tedious process.

In 1846, Parliament formed a Gauge Commission to solve this problem. In its Gauge Act of 1846, the Commission conceded that although the broad-gauge trains maintained a higher speed and smoother ride, the majority of the country used the smaller, Stephenson gauge; thus, the Stephenson gauge was

By employing a wider-gauged track than was the standard, the Great Western Railway became the fastest and smoothest riding railway in the world. Unfortunately, problems arose when the wide-gauge track met up with the standard narrow gauge track. Each car had to be lifted off its wide-gauge chassis and attached to a narrow gauge (below). The last wide gauge train (above) pulled out of Paddington station on May 20, 1892.

National Railway Museum/York, England

In 1846, Parliament ruled that the narrow gauge, developed by George Stephenson, be adopted as the national standard. The Great Western Railway, however, resisted making the conversion until 1868, and even then, did not complete the changeover until 1892.

National Railway Museum/York, England

In a mere fifty years, the steam-powered railroad became the major mode of passenger and freight transportation in the world. The Railroad Age had begun and Great Britain was its leader.

adopted as the standard. The government, however, balked at forcing the GWR to convert. Prime Minister Sir Robert Peel was afraid that, since Parliament originally authorized the GWR's broad gauge, Brunel would have grounds to charge the government for the costs of conversion. As a compromise, the GWR laid a third rail to make its line a mixed-gauge railway.

By 1868, competition forced the GWR to begin the final conversion to the standard 4-foot-8 gauge. Even so, the final broad gauge train was not taken out of service until 1892.

Europe

Unlike the United States and even Great Britain, countries on the European continent proceeded with their railroad development in a relatively orderly fashion. The unbridled competition between private railroad companies in England and the United States was averted in Europe through better planning and government involvement.

Leading the way to rail expansion in Europe was Belgium. This small country had become independent in 1831 and was eager to

be recognized by the rest of the world. Belgium saw the railroads as an opportunity to make Antwerp an internationally competitive economic center. In a law passed in May 1834, the young Belgian government decided to create a state-owned rail system, the first state-run system anywhere.

Using British track and engines and even hiring the renowned George Stephenson as a consultant, Belgium laid the first track of their rail system in 1836. The Belgian railroad, however, was not immediately profitable because it was competing with an extremely advanced water transport system. Eventually most of the Belgian Rail system was sold to private companies, but was later bought back by the government in 1926, because of the fear of foreign takeover.

Germany also jumped onto the railway bandwagon in 1834 when Ludwig I approved construction of the Ludwigsbahn, a railway from Nuremburg to Furth. Using locomotives built by George and Robert Stephenson, the Ludwigsbahn opened for passenger service on December 7, 1835. By 1850 Germany had laid nearly 4,000 route miles (6,400 kilometers) of track. Despite the fact that Germany was made of many independent states, these rail lines were the best planned and most economically built railways in the world—made at nearly half the cost per mile of British and American track. In the early stages of development, German railways, like most others around the world, were dependent on British locomotives and technology, but by 1841 Germany's greatest locomotive builder, August Borsig, began turning out the first German-built locomotives.

Because of a primarily agricultural economy and a good system of roads and highways, France was slow to develop a railway system. When the country did seem ready to begin building railways, a lengthy debate over state or private ownership caused a further delay. The very first railways were begrudgingly handed over to private enterprises, but the debate was far from over. In 1840 the Paris-Orleans Company was overcome by financial difficulties and had to be bailed out by the French government.

The French Assembly soon came to realize that an efficient railway system was not possible without direct government involvement. This led to the Railway Law of 1842, which planned for a network of trunk routes centered on Paris. The ownership of the lines would be split between state and private railroad companies. The state would be responsible for planning the location of the lines as well as the construction of the track bed and any necessary bridges and viaducts. The companies, in turn, would be responsible for laying the track and erecting any stations or buildings that were necessary.

This joint ownership system helped the French avoid the problems the British were finding themselves in with a mass of competing trunk lines following virtually the same routes. Strategically planned and extremely well built, the French trunk lines are still among the best in the world for high-speed rail service.

Although France entered the railway business later than other European nations, today France operates some of the world's fastest trains.

CHAPTER FOUR

THE AGE OF LUXURIOUS TRAVEL

IN THE EARLY DAYS OF PASSENGER TRAINS, VERY LIT-
tle consideration was given to the comfort of the traveler.
The very first passenger cars were nothing more than open
wooden wagons, without seats. A roof was the first conces-
sion to the comfort and well-being of the passenger. This
was quickly followed by wooden benches and then, eventually, cushioned seats.

Early railroad entrepreneurs hoped to gain attention to
their new form of transportation by attracting the business
of royalty and the noblesse. To do this they produced a number of elegant parlor cars for kings and princes and then
publicized any trips the royalty made. These elegant rail
cars, however, were limited to private use. The general public still had to suffer cramped seats, a lack of lavatories, and
improper ventilation during bumpy excursions over the
iron rails.

For short distances, the uncomfortable conditions did not
pose too many problems. The trains made enough stops for
passengers to relieve themselves and stretch out their mus-
cle cramps and sore necks. By the 1860s, however, rail trips

In the very early days of the railroads, very few concessions were given to the passenger's comfort. Trains were little more than glorified stage coaches, as can be seen in this 1831 photo of the **DeWitt Clinton,** *the first passenger train to operate in the state of New York. As train rides became longer, however, passengers began to demand more. Eventually, the rail companies added such amenities as cushioned seats, stove heat, and finally, the famous sleeping cars.*

were getting longer, and rail travel in general was getting a reputation for being a trip through purgatory. Finally, with the completion of America's first transcontinental route, it became evident that a few more concessions would have to be made to passenger comfort.

In 1859, a young entrepreneur named George Mortimer Pullman drew up plans for a practical and comfortable sleeping car. Pullman was born in upstate New York on March 1, 1831, about the same time rail travel in the United States began. As a young man, Pullman worked in his brother's cabinet-making shop, which gave him the skills he would later use in his own enterprises.

After moving to Chicago, Pullman submitted his first plans to the Chicago & Alton Railroad. Although they were initially unenthused about Pullman's ideas, they nonetheless provided him with two rail cars and the services of a Chicago & Alton woodworker named Leonard G. Seibert. The two men worked together and converted the first of the two day cars into a comfortable and luxurious (for the times) sleeping car.

According to Seibert, "Into this car, we got ten sleeping-car sections, a linen closet, and two tiny washrooms, one at each end. Remodelling cost about $1000 a car. We had no blueprints to go by. Mr. Pullman and I personally worked out the details as we came to them.

*In 1859, a young innovator and former cabinet-maker named George Mortimer Pullman drew up plans for a practical and comfortable sleeping car. Pullman's first car (opposite page) was primitive compared to the more elaborate cars he developed in years to come. An upper level of beds lowered from the ceiling, while the backs of the chairs reclined to form a lower level of beds. Pullman's cars did not become popular, however, until the **Pioneer** was used as part of President Lincoln's funeral train.*

The cars were upholstered in plush, heated in cold weather by box stoves, and each was mounted on four iron-wheeled trucks."

Beds hung from the ceiling of the car and were lowered at night with a system of ropes and pulleys. In addition, the backs of the seats could be lowered to form the base for a lower level of beds. To facilitate the transition from day travel to night travel, Pullman hired his own crew of porters, which later became an American symbol of customer service.

Pullman's first two cars went into service on September 1, 1859; they met with moderate success. Encouraged by their first two prototypes, Pullman and Seibert set out to make a much more elaborate car. Dubbed the *Pioneer,* this elegant rail car was lined with polished black walnut and decorated with crystal chandeliers and marble washbasins. As beautiful as the *Pioneer* was, it did have one major problem: It was 2.5 feet (seventy-six centimeters) taller and one foot (thirty centimeters) wider than any rail car ever used on American railroads. Its extended size made it too big to fit under many bridges or alongside most rail stations, and the rail companies were unwilling to alter their railside structures just to accommodate Pullman. It seemed as if the Pullman sleeping car were going to come to a swift end.

The assassination of President Lincoln in 1865, however, provided just the break that Pullman needed. The state of Illinois requested that the *Pioneer* be used as part of Lincoln's funeral train. The Chicago & Alton had to quickly alter their tracks before the funeral train's trip across the state. Soon after the funeral, General Grant decided to use the *Pioneer* for a trip from Detroit to his home town of Galena, Michigan, and other railroads were similarly forced to alter their tracks.

The publicity generated by these two events helped Pullman cultivate a healthy business, and in 1867 he officially named his company the Pullman Palace Car Company. By that year there were fifty Pullman sleepers in operation across the midwest and demand was growing. Always eager to expand, Pullman designed the *President,* the first "hotel car," for the Great Western Railway of Canada. The *President* was a standard Pullman sleeper with the added luxury of a small kitchen at one end. In order to expand food service, Pullman developed the first full-length dining car named the *Delmonico,* after a famous New York restaurateur.

By the end of the nineteenth century, the luxury train was a crucial component of the North American rail system. A typical first class, or "limited," train would include a barber shop; a club or smoking car complete with a multivolume library; a parlor with ornate paneling and plush armchairs; and a three-star dining car, which offered fare that equalled that of the finest restaurants in the country. Overseeing all of this opulence was an ornately uniformed staff, predominantly black, of Pullman porters, whose duty it was to wait on the passengers hand and foot.

DINING SERVICE

NEW YORK CENTRAL LINES

HORS D'OEUVRES—Green Olives 25   India Relish 20

Ripe Olives 25   Hearts of Celery 35   Sliced Tomatoes 45

Melon Mangoes 25   Midget Gherkins 25

French Sardines in Olive Oil 75

Our Specialties

BISQUE OF NEW TOMATOES AND PEAS,
Cup......................30   Tureen......................45

CONSOMME, HOT..............Cup 25;   Jellied Cup 40

CLAM BROTH...............................(Cup) 30

FRESH LAKE TROUT, *Broiled, Parsley Butter, Potatoes Saute, String Beans Fleurette*..................95

DELAWARE SHAD ROE,
Country Bacon, Potato Chips..............................95

GRILLED COUNTRY HAM,
Creamed New Spinach, New Potatoes..................95

LOIN OF LAMB IN CASSEROLE *with String Beans in Butter, Parisienne Potatoes*..................95

FRIED SPRING CHICKEN IN BUTTER, *Bacon and New Potatoes in Cream*..........................1.25

SMALL SIRLOIN GRILLED, *with Chives, Country Bacon and French Fried Potatoes*........1.25

EGGS ON HEARTS OF LETTUCE,
Tartare Sauce 85

NEW POTATOES IN CREAM.......................40

VELOUTE OF NEW SPINACH, *with Egg* 45

LETTUCE AND CUCUMBER SALAD,
Russian Dressing...45

HOT TEA BISCUITS, *with Honey*.........................35

FRENCH PANCAKE with *Marmalade*..................35

STRAWBERRY SHORT CAKE *with Cream* 45

HOME MADE PIE...25

GRAPE FRUIT (Iced) HALF 35

IMPORTED ROQUEFORT CHEESE
Toasted Crackers...40

Scrambled Eggs with Chopped Ham 75
Kippered Herring on Toast, Scrambled Eggs..65
Ham and Fried Eggs 80   Bacon and Fried Eggs 80   Ham 80; (Reduced Portion) 45
Bacon 80; (Reduced Portion) 45   Baked Beans, Hot or Cold 45
Home Fried Potatoes 30   French Fried Potatoes 35   Hashed Brown Potatoes 35
Hot Asparagus, Drawn Butter 50   Asparagus Vinaigrette 50
Refugee String Beans 30   Early June Peas 30

EGGS—Omelette, Plain 60;   Ham, Bacon, Jelly or Asparagus Omelette 75
Boiled (2) 35   Scrambled 40;   with Mushrooms 75   Fried (2) 40

SALADS, DESSERTS, ETC.—Pineapple and Cheese Salad, French Dressing.....................45
Lettuce and Tomato Salad 45
Cream Cheese with Toasted Rye Bread and Red Currant Jelly....................................40
Hawaiian Pineapple 35   Preserved Figs with Cream 50   Strawberry Preserves 35
French Vanilla Ice Cream 30   Assorted Cake 25   Orange Marmalade 35
Rye or Graham Bread 15; Toasted 20   Bread and Butter 15   Toast 20
Tea (Pot for 1) 25   Coffee (Pot for 1) 25   Cocoa (Pot for 1) 25   Postum (Pot for 1) 25
Milk (Individual Bottle) 20   Malted Milk (Pot for One) 25

Above Portions Per Person Only

An extra charge of 25 cents per person will be made for meals served out of dining car

Passengers are respectfully informed that no verbal orders for meals will be accepted, and are requested to pay the punched total only on presentation of check on which the order is written.

Please see Steward in charge of car, if the service is not entirely to your satisfaction.

J. R. SMART, Manager, Dining Service, Cincinnati, Ohio

5-B-2

As train travel became popular among the elite classes, first-class travel became more and more extravagant. Most luxury trains included an observation car (above) complete with library, and a dining car serving four-star fare. The menu on the opposite page is from a dining car on Vanderbilt's New York Central Line.

Demand for Pullman cars became so great that in order to keep up with production, Pullman formed his own industrial town—Pullman, Illinois. A combined manufacturing and residential development, Pullman, Illinois was the first planned industrial community in the United States. Although Pullman dubbed this community his model city, the living and working conditions for his 14,000 employees, most of whom were black, were less than ideal. They lived in wooden shacks that lacked running water and adequate sani-

tation facilities, and a large part of their already low salaries was deducted for rent and food from the company store.

During the recession of 1893, 4,000 Pullman employees were laid off and the others were forced to accept severe wage cuts, even though the Pullman Company was pulling in revenues that topped $16 million a year. The Chicago branch of the American Railroad Union (ARU), under the leadership of Eugene V. Debs, tried to force Pullman to arbitrate the grievances of his workers. The steadfast Pull-

To pamper his passengers further, George Pullman hired a staff of Pullman Porters for each of his Palace Cars. The Pullman Porter (right) became a symbol of luxury and service. By middle of the twentieth century, rail companies such as The New York Central tried to lure new passengers with new diesel-powered, high-speed trains. Opposite page is a 1948 advertisement introducing the 20th Century Limited, one of New York Central's "Dreamliner" fleet.

World Premiere!

the New 20th Century Limited

First of New York Central's New Dreamliner Fleet

New **Lookout Lounge**—Modern setting for the club-like sociability that's long been a *Century* tradition.

New – from its streamlined Diesel to its raised "Lookout Lounge"...

New **King-Size Diner**—So spacious it needs a separate kitchen car! Smart designing gives each table privacy plus a perfect outlook. There's a festive feel about the *Century* dinner hour and a sense of being served with distinction.

New **1948 Century Rooms**—Whether you travel in a roomette, bedroom or with a party in a suite, you can work or relax in air-conditioned privacy by day—then sleep the miles away by night on Central's smooth Water Level Route.

NEW YORK CENTRAL
The Water Level Route — You Can Sleep

NEW YORK CENTRAL SYSTEM

BETWEEN THE HEART OF CHICAGO AND THE HEART OF NEW YORK

Vacation overnight aboard the new Century. Arrive refreshed —with no business time lost.

© Christopher Bain

© Christopher Bain

Comfort and elegance was at its highest in the lavish Pullman and Wagon-Lits cars; however, not all train travel was so extravagant. Passengers had a choice of first, second, or third class travel. Of course, the ultra-rich often opted for buying their own personal rail cars for the ultimate in conspicuous travel.

man refused, stating emphatically, "There is nothing to arbitrate."

Pullman successfully crushed the strike in 1891 and maintained totalitarian control over his employees; however, the struggle had an adverse affect on his health and he died of a heart attack three years later. Upon hearing the news of Pullman's death, labor activist Eugene Debs commented. "Death is a social democrat. The time was when Mr. Pullman had nothing to arbitrate. Now comes the time when Death has nothing to arbitrate."

The Wagon-Lits Company and The Orient Express

In 1868, George Nagelmackers, heir to a Belgian banking fortune, traveled to America, where he was overwhelmed by the luxury and elegance of the Pullman sleepers. British and European trains had previously experimented with a few primitive bunk-car arrangements, but none came close to matching the opulence of the Pullman Palace Cars. These cars made long-term train travel in the United States a pleasurable experience. Nagelmackers realized that Europe represented a huge untapped market for elegant transcontinental service.

Upon his return home, Nagelmackers approached many European Railroad companies with his ideas for a practical sleeping car. Unable to gain financial backers, Nagelmack-

© Christopher Bain

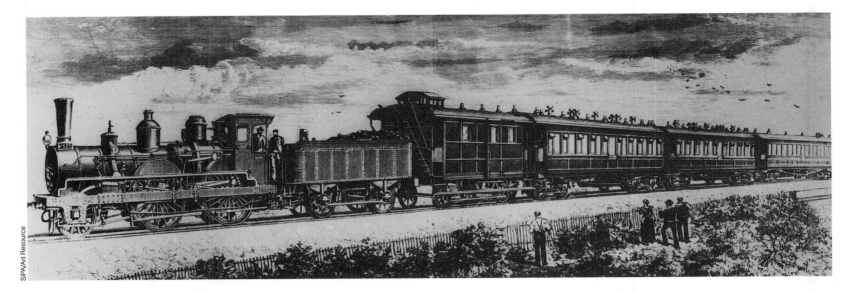

ers used his own money to convert a few small cars into Pullman-style sleepers. His sleepers enjoyed moderate success on the Ostend-Cologne line; however, without adequate financial backing Nagelmackers faced bankruptcy. Just as it seemed that his fledgling enterprise was nearing its end, in stepped a United States Army engineer named Colonel William d'Alton Mann.

Mann had also been trying to enter the sleeping-car market, but was wary of competing with Pullman in America. After an unsuccessful attempt at entering the British market, Mann looked toward Continental Europe, where he gained the acquaintance of Nagelmackers. The two joined forces and began producing the Mann Boudoir Sleeping Cars.

Nagelmackers used his marketing skills to gain a long-term contract with the French railway system. He then convinced the Prince of Wales to use a boudoir car for his well-publicized trip to Russia. Within a year the business began to prosper.

In 1876, Nagelmackers bought out Mann and formed the Compagnie Internationale des Wagons-Lits et des Grands Express Europeans, or more commonly the Wagons-Lits Company. An essential part of the new Wagons-Lits trains was an elegant dining car that served first-class meals. Nagelmackers's venture into luxurious travel was an immediate success with the European upper class. By the end of the century more than 500 Wagons-Lits diners and sleepers were being

L'Orient Express, Train De Luxe De La Compagnie Des Wagon-Lits, *more simply known as the* **Orient Express,** *was the brainchild of Belgian banker-turned-railroad-man George Nagelmackers.*

used on 90,000 miles (144,000 kilometers) of European tracks.

Nagelmackers made further history in 1883 with the birth of the European *train de luxe*. The *Orient Express* was a lavish passenger train that traveled across the entire European continent to Constantinople, the gateway to Asia. Made up solely of Wagons-Lits cars, the *Orient Express* became the most famous luxury train in history.

From its very first run, the *Orient Express* epitomized the romance of European train travel. The original train had three passenger coaches designed for the utmost in grandeur. The walls and dividers were carved from in-

laid teak, black walnut, and mahogany. The beds had silk sheets and the lavatories had marble bowls and gold plumbing. Behind the passenger coaches was a ladies' parlor car and a men's smoking room, complete with library.

The dining car, however, was the most ornate car on the *Express*. The hand-carved wooden interior was decorated with colorful paintings and crystal chandeliers. All of the tables were set with the finest linens and sterling silver dinnerware. The royalty and aristocracy that rode on the *Orient Express* usually donned full evening dress for dinner and were often entertained by live music. A separate car was needed just to hold all of the

*The most famous of all luxury trains was the glamorous **Orient Express**. Complete with black walnut, teak, and mahogany walls; stately, private sleeping rooms; and overstuffed leather chairs, the **Orient Express** epitomized romantic travel and inspired countless writers and artists.*

*Following page: Today, the Nostalgic **Orient Express** runs from Zurich to Istanbul and still uses some of the original rolling stock from the 1920s. Here, the **Orient Express** waits in a station in Yugoslavia.*

food, wine, champagne, and brandy that would be consumed on the long journey.

Over the years, this hotel on wheels inspired literally hundreds of authors—from Agatha Cristie to Graham Greene—to use the famous train as a backdrop for their books. The original *Orient Express* went out of business in 1977. Today, however, train enthusiasts can ride on the *Nostalgic Orient Express,* which runs from Zurich to Istanbul and uses some of the original rail cars that were used in the 1920s.

Another of the famous trains de luxe was the Trans-Siberian Express. Traveling from western Russia to China, this Wagon-Lits train was considered by many to be the most elegant of all trains. With the Communist revolution in Russia in 1917, the Wagon-Lits involvement in the Trans-Siberian Express came to an end.

In addition to the *Orient Express,* Wagon-Lits Company established many other luxury trains, the two most famous of which traveled through Tsarist Russia. The St. Petersburg-Vienna-Nice-Cannes train was considered by many to be the grandest *train de luxe* of the prewar era. Not far behind, however, was the *Trans-Siberian Express,* which traveled across Russia to distant China. With the communist revolution, however, the Wagon-Lits involvement in both of these rail lines came to an abrupt end.

After the deaths of both Nagelmackers and Pullman, the Wagon-Lits Company merged with the European Pullman Company, which already had a strong hold on the British and Italian markets. For forty years these two companies dominated passenger train travel all over the world. Eventually, however, the rich abandoned the leisurely pace of train travel for the swift transport of the airplane. By the 1950s, the age of the luxury train had passed, and with it went much of the romance and allure of train travel in general.

TRACKS THROUGH THE WILDERNESS

THE RAILROAD BOOM OF THE LATE NINETEENTH and early twentieth century played a critical role in the economic development of every country in the world. Without this new and efficient form of transportation the industrial revolution would not have been able to progress as quickly as it did. Industry developed a voracious appetite for raw materials and new markets, which the railroads helped to feed.

In order to fully understand the true impact of the steam locomotive on world history, it is important to explore the iron rail's advancement through the wilderness. The railroad industry helped shape the boundaries of the world. New territories were explored, new cities were founded, and previously fragmented countries were united. The Canadian Pacific, the Trans-Siberian, and the Alaskan railroads all forged their ways through rough, unforgiving terrain and into the history books.

The Canadian Pacific Railway

While England, the United States, and most of continental Europe were fervently laying track in the midst of the railroad boom of the mid 1800s, the Canadian provinces were much slower to realize the potential of the iron rail. By the 1850s, the United States had more than 10,000 miles (16,000 kilometers) of track in operation, and the number was increasing daily. Canada, on the other hand, had less than 100 miles (160 kilometers).

Canada's slow start in the railway race can be partially attributed to the fact that, as late as the 1840s, the majority of its population was concentrated in the east along the Atlantic coast, the basin of the St Lawrence River, and the northern shore of the Great Lakes. Except for the Pacific coast, where a colony, British Columbia, had sprung up, there had been no great western expansion in Canada like there had been in the United States.

The huge section of land between the Hudson Bay and the Rocky Mountains known as Rupert's Land was under the control of the powerful Hudson River Company. In order to retain control of the land, the Hudson River Company portrayed Rupert's Land as an extension of the great American desert, a wasteland that was good for nothing except fur trading.

The first proposal for a railway across Canada was presented in 1849 by British Major Robert Carmichael-Smyth, who saw a Canadian transcontinental railway as a way of providing a vital link between Hong Kong and Great Britain. It should be noted that six years earlier Great Britain had taken control of Hong Kong, and this Chinese port city had become Britain's major source of silk, porcelain, tea, and other exotic oriental goods. Carmichael-Smyth thought that goods could be shipped to the colony of British Columbia, transported by train across Canada by rail, and then shipped on to England. He maintained that this route would be much quicker and cheaper than the current methods of shipping goods around Africa by boat or across Asia by wagon.

While Carmichael-Smyth's idea sounded good, it was not very well thought-out and did not take into account Canada's formidable natural obstacles, such as the Canadian Shield and the Rocky Mountains. After minor consideration, the proposal was shelved.

By the late 1840s, European immigrants began to flock to Canada. Canadian capitalists and government officials realized that in order for Canada to grow economically, it had to grow physically as well. The logical choice for expansion was Rupert's Land. By this time the Hudson River Company's control was beginning to wane, so in 1857, the Canadian Assembly sent an expedition headed by Simon Dawson into the Northwest Territory to assess the agricultural potential of the area, as well as the possibility of a viable transportation link. In the same year, the British sent an ex-

By the mid-nineteenth century, the United States had more than 10,000 miles (16,000 km) of track in operation. Canada, on the other hand, had less than 100 miles (160 km). One of the priorities of the new Dominion of Canada was to build a transcontinental railroad linking the west to the east. Canada's harsh weather and rough terrain made such a railroad a difficult engineering challenge.

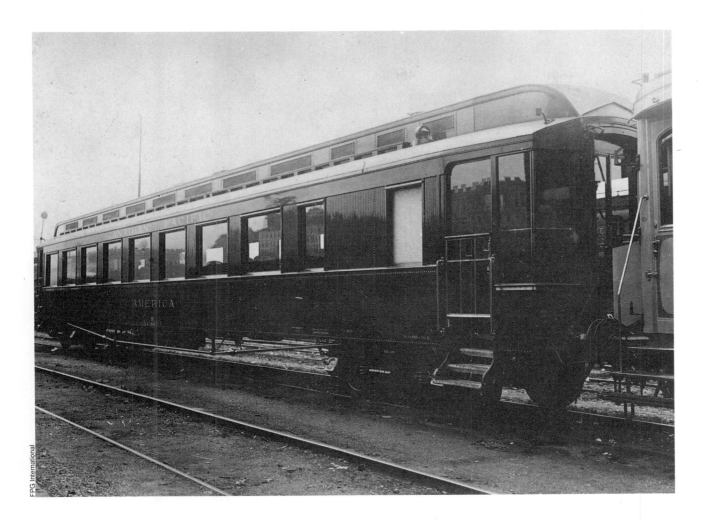

In 1928, the Canadian National Railways introduced the world's first diesel-electric locomotive (below). Canadian Pacific Railroad upgraded its first-class travel with the purchase of its first Pullman car, the America.

FPG International

American Association of Railroads

Snow created a significant obstacle to the operation of the Canadian Pacific Railroad. Several sections of the line had to be protected with sheds to keep snow from drifting onto the tracks.

pedition of their own into the area, headed by Captain John Palliser.

The Canadian expedition concluded that the Red and Assiniboine valleys, as well as the "Fertile Belt of the North Saskatchewan Valley," possessed great agricultural potential and could maintain a sizable settlement. Palliser also concluded that the Northwest could support a large population and suggested a railroad be built up the Saskatchewan Valley and through the Yellowhead Pass.

The positive results of the two expeditions widened an already growing Canadian interest in the area. At the same time, just south of the border, American settlers were streaming

west. Americans settled the Oregon territory, forcing the British out, and the territory of Minnesota. With the formation of St. Paul in Minnesota, Americans gained control of the upper Mississippi and Red River valleys, while establishing substantial steamboat and rail connections. This extensive American settling, combined with the completion of the first transcontinental railroad in the United States in 1869, made the Canadians extremely nervous.

In 1869, the two-year-old Dominion of Canada had just gained control of Rupert's Land from the Hudson River Company; however, John A. Macdonald, Canada's first prime minister, became increasingly worried that the United States would begin to expand north into the colony of British Columbia, which was not yet under Canadian control. Macdonald envisioned Canada as a powerful transcontinental nation, linked by a trail of iron from coast to coast.

In 1870, delegates from British Columbia and Canada met in Ottawa to negotiate a union. In order to get to Ottawa, the British Columbian delegation had to travel from Victoria to San Francisco by steamboat. Then they took the Central Pacific and Union Pacific railroads across the United States, and then had to travel back up north by rail to Ottawa. If they were to make the journey through Canada they would have been forced to travel by a combination of stage coach, dogsled, canoe, and steamboat. It was not surprising that one of the main conditions of the union hinged on the completion of a transcontinental railway. According to the agreement, which was signed in July 1871, the Dominion had to begin work on the railway in two years and complete it within ten years.

Eager to get the project going, Macdonald appointed Sandford Fleming to the position of chief engineer of the Pacific Railway Survey. His job was to find the most feasible and economical route through 2,500 miles (4,000 kilometers) of Canadian swamps, grasslands, and mountain ranges. In 1872, the government approved Fleming's route around the north shore of Lake Superior, up the North Saskatchewan River Valley, and through the Yellowhead Pass. In 1873, Macdonald contracted the whole project out to a private company headed by Canadian shipping magnate, Sir Hugh Allan.

Allan and his newly incorporated Canadian Pacific Railway Company lasted a mere two months. In November 1873, the Liberal Opposition Party made it public that Macdonald had received substantial financial support from Allan during the 1872 elections, and that the contract with the Canadian Pacific Railway was a result of corrupt ties between the two. As proof, the Liberal Party produced a telegram from Macdonald to Allan: "Immediate, private, I must have another ten thousand. Will be the last time of calling. Do not fail me. Answer today." The scandal forced the Macdonald government to resign, and with it, the Canadian Pacific Railroad Company died.

The railway project was further delayed when a severe recession strained the fragile Canadian economy. Macdonald's successor, Alexander Mackenzie, signed the Canadian Pacific Railroad Act in 1874 in an attempt to appease the angered British Columbians. The 1874 act, however, took a much slower approach to building the railroad than Macdonald had originally foreseen. Under the new plan the railway would be built piece by piece, with contracts awarded to several companies instead of just one. In the first four years of construction only sixty-three miles (100 kilometers) of track were lain, and track

Many trains were equipped with large snow-plows to help in the never-ending battle against the elements.

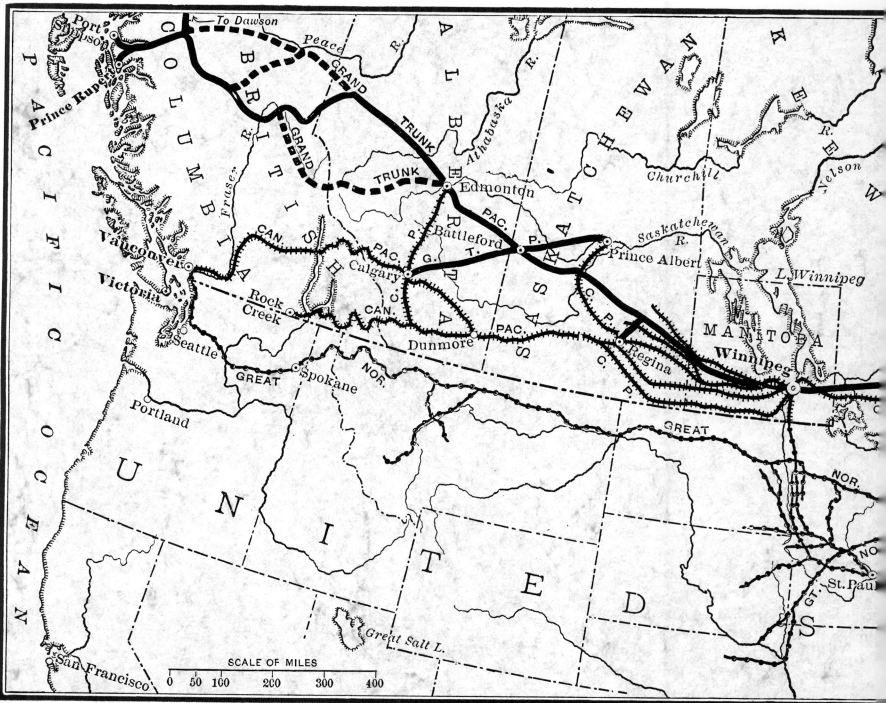

The building of a transcontinental railroad in Canada posed many serious engineering problems. The railroad had to traverse thousands of miles of frozen tundra, rocky ledges, and jagged mountain peaks.

laying in Western Canada did not even begin until the fall of 1877.

By 1878, the Canadian depression had deepened and Mackenzie was run out of office and replaced by Macdonald, who had gained back the public's favor under an aggressive campaign of Canadian nationalism, western settlement, and swift completion of the transcontinental railway. In 1880, Macdonald signed a contract with a group headed by George Stephens, president of the Bank of Montreal. This newly formed railroad syndicate included James J. Hill and Richard B. Angus of the Manitoba and Minneapolis Railroad, Duncan McIntyre of the Canada Central Railroad, and a New York financier by the name of John S. Kennedy.

In return for building the railway, the syndicate was to receive $25 million and twenty-five million acres of land "fairly fit for settlement." In addition, they gained control of other railways which were either completed or under construction, as well as a guarantee that the new railway would be without com-

petitors for twenty years. The new Canadian Pacific Railroad Company (CPR) was incorporated on February 16, 1881. Westward construction began on May 2, 1881, taking a southerly route that avoided Yellowhead Pass. Using a similar tactic as the American transcontinental railroad, the CPR started simultaneous construction from the east and west.

Initial progress from the east was slow until James Hill brought in William C. Van Horne to oversee construction of the project. Much to the surprise of surveyors and engineers, the Ontario section of track proved to be very difficult. The line had to traverse the rocky shore of Lake Superior, as well as deep swamp that swallowed tons of landfill and miles of track. Despite these obstacles, Van Horne vowed to lay 500 miles (800 kilometers) of track in 1882. During his first month as overseer, Van Horne laid more than sixty miles (ninety-six kilometers) of track, setting a phenomenal single-day record of 6.38 miles (10.2 kilometers). Using 12,000 men and 2,000 teams of horses, Van Horne was able to

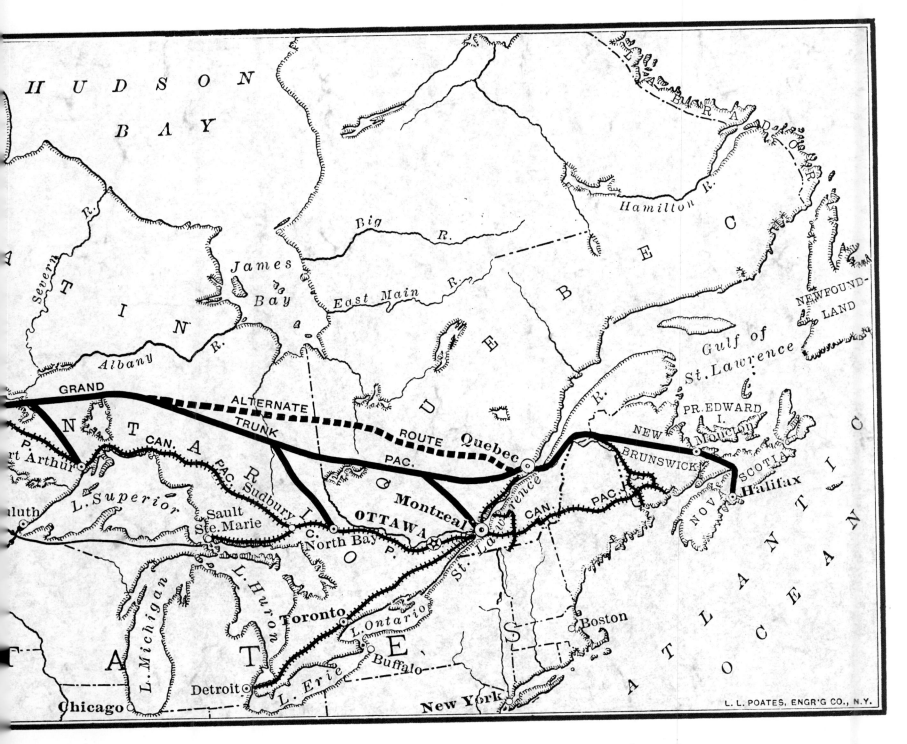

reach Calgary by August 1883. In a little over a year Van Horne and his men laid 675 miles (1,080 kilometers) of track. The quickly laid track, however, was left unballasted and sometimes out of grade. Follow-up crews worked behind the "end of steel," improving and leveling the track as they went.

From the west, a crew made up mostly of Chinese workers, under the direction of Andrew Onderdonk, laid track eastward from Port Moody towards Eagle Pass. Traversing rocky ledges and river banks, this section was the most dangerous of all on the transcontinental line. Nearly 600 workers were killed by rock slides and epidemics, a cost of four men per mile of track. Upon reaching Eagle Pass, Onderdonk and his crew sat and waited for Van Horne to traverse the 5,329-foot (1,624-meter) high Kicking Horse Pass through the Rocky Mountains, and the Continental Divide, the dangerous 4,300-foot (1,310-kilometer) high Rogers Pass through the Selkirks, named after American survey engineer Major A.B. Rogers.

In order to expedite construction and avoid costly tunneling, the Kicking Horse Pass section traveled down a 7.5 mile (twelve-kilometer) hill known simply as the Big Hill. Possessing a gradient of one in twenty-two, the Big Hill was the steepest ever attempted for a main line. Once the line was opened, it would take four large steam engines to pull an average train up this hill. When going down the hill engineers had to maintain a speed of no more than six miles (ten kilometers) per hour, with safety stops every two miles (three kilometers) to inspect the brakes. In 1909, the Big Hill was replaced by two spiral tunnels with a lesser gradient.

Rogers Pass, on the other hand, did not have a huge gradient problem, but it was susceptible to avalanches and snow drifts. In order to keep the snow from falling on the track, more than five miles (eight kilometers) of snow sheds were built. Rogers Pass was eventually bypassed in 1916 with a five-mile (eight-kilometer) tunnel under Mount Sir Donald.

In a small, unpretentious ceremony on November 7, 1885, Donald Smith drove in the last spike (it was iron) at Craigellachie in Eagle Pass. In front of a small group of railway executives, Van Horne made a simple speech: "All I can say is that the work has been done well in every way.... The last spike will be just as good an iron one as there is between Montreal and Vancouver, and anyone who wants to see it...will have to pay full fare." On the same day, a few miles down the track, the workers staged their own last spike ceremony.

The next day, the first train to travel from Canadian coast to Canadian coast pulled into

Today, Canadian Pacific Limited is one of the largest and most diversified companies in Canada. In addition to railways, now known as CP Rail, the company is involved in sea and air transportation, hotels, real estate, and financial services.

Port Moody. The railway officially opened on November 11, 1885, at 8:00 p.m. when the *Pacific Express* left Montreal for Port Moody.

With the opening of the CPR, there came settlement in the Canadian prairies. This expansion enabled the CPR to triple its rail mileage, to over 30,000 (48,000 kilometers), by the beginning of World War I. By the 1890s, CPR had diversified its interests into the transatlantic and Great Lakes steamship business. This led the British Government to contract the CPR to provide mail service between Hong Kong and London. With the addition of three luxury ocean liners in 1891—*Empress*

of India, Empress of Japan, and *Empress of China*—the Canadian Pacific Company began passenger service to the Orient, advertising "Around the World in 80 Days—$610."

Today, the Canadian Pacific has assets that exceed $8.5 billion in land, sea, and air transportation, as well as hotels, real estate, and financial services. In 1971, the parent company was renamed Canadian Pacific Limited, with the railway known as CP Rail or the Canadian Pacific. It currently operates about 1,300 diesel locomotives and 65,000 freight cars over 30,000 miles (48,000 kilometers) of track in Canada and the United States.

Following page: A Via Rail passenger train rolls down the tracks near Banff, Alberta.

The Canadian Pacific Railroad winds through some of the most scenic country in all of North America. CP Rail currently has about 30,000 miles (48,000 km) of track in operation.

The Trans-Siberian Railroad

The Russian press hailed the trans-Siberian railroad as "the fairest jewel in the crown of the Tsars." The British press was not so enthusiastic. They described the new Russian railroad as "rusty streaks of iron through the vastness of nothing to the extremities of nowhere." Extending more than 6,000 miles (9,600 kilometers), from the Ural Mountains to the Sea of Japan at Vladivostok, the trans-Siberian railway remains the longest continuous railway in the world. It provides an indispensable link between European Russia and the huge, resource-rich Asian landmass to the east.

In 1579, the Strogonov family, traders in east Russia, sent an army of about eight hundred, headed by an outlaw named Yermak, into western Siberia to capture Sibir, the Tartar capital. By doing so, Yermak won a pardon from the Tsar and the Tsar gained new territories to the West. Throughout the seventeenth century, all of northern Siberia came under Russian control as fur traders explored its farthest regions. Still largely unsettled in the beginning of the eighteenth century, Siberia became notorious for its prison camps when Peter the Great started the tradition of sending political exiles there.

While this huge territory was technically under Russian control, there was no good system of communication with or transportation to the area. A few military ports sprang up on the eastern coast, but the Tsar had no real way of protecting Russia's interests in the area. The quickest and most effective way to travel into Siberia in winter was still by sled. The problem with this was that Siberian winters were so cold that frostbite and hypothermia were constant threats. Whether traveling in the winter by sled, or in the summer by wagon or horseback, the journey through Siberia was a long and arduous one. Just how long the journey took is depicted in the story of the Kamchatka virgins.

According to legend, in the early eighteenth century Empress Petrovna invited three beautiful Kamchatka virgins to visit her at St. Petersburg. Kamchatka is a remote peninsula just opposite Alaska's southernmost tip, nine thousand miles (14,000 kilometers) away from St. Petersburg. Throughout their journey, the three women were to be escorted by an Imperial officer. By the time they reached Irkutsk, the trading center of eastern

Siberia, each of the "virgins" had given birth to a child fathered by the Imperial guard. This officer was replaced by another, more trustworthy chaperone. By the time the three women reached St. Petersburg, however, each had given birth to a second child, this time fathered by the second military escort.

Throughout most of the nineteenth century, Siberia was considered a frozen wasteland and went virtually ignored by the tsars.

This disregard for Russia's eastern territories was epitomized when Alexander II sold Alaska to the United States for two cents an acre. Ironically, it was not a Russian but an American named Perry McDonough Collins who first recognized Siberia's potential and proposed a railway through the area.

Born in Hyde Park, New York, in 1813, Collins studied law in New York City, worked for a steamship company in New Orleans, Louisi-

ana, and eventually went to San Francisco during the gold rush of 1849. While in San Francisco, Collins developed an obsessive interest in Siberia after reading a number of articles and books on the area. He believed that Siberia was an almost limitless source of natural resources and that it possessed a great "value to the commerce of the world, if it could only obtain an easy outlet to the ocean." Collins saw the Amur River as a potential channel for United States trade.

In 1856, Collins traveled to Washington to get support for a trip to Siberia. On March 24 of the same year he was appointed Commercial Agent of the United States at the Amoor River. With the support of the United States government, Collins immediately set sail for St. Petersburg, the first stop on his journey to Siberia.

Collins and an American companion referred to only as Mr. Peyton left for Irkutsk by sled on December 3, 1856. Despite winter temperatures that ranged from ten degrees above zero to fifty degrees below, Collins and Peyton left St. Petersburg with a positive attitude. In his book *A Voyage Down the Amoor,* Collins wrote, "In fact, we had determined to make the journey a frolic, intending to have a good time of it, or at least the best possible under the circumstances."

Despite the many accidents and delays associated with winter travel, Collins and Peyton reached Irkutsk on January 7, 1857. They covered the 3,500 miles (5,600 kilometers) in 35

days, using more than 700 horses and 200 drivers en route.

After two months of courting the Irkutsk dignitaries, Collins began the second leg of his journey down the Ingoda, Shilka, and Amur Rivers. He reached the Pacific Port of Nikolayevsk on July 10, 1857, 6,000 miles (9,600 kilometers) from his starting point in St. Petersburg. Collins first proposed a railroad system across Siberia in a letter sent to Michael S. Korsakov, then the governor of the Transbaikal territory. In his letter he stated: "The Amoor must become in the hands of Russia a very important country, through which a great trade will flow, opening Siberia to the commerce of the world.... Building this road [will] make the heart of Siberia easily accessible to commerce, so that her products can be quickly and readily exchanged or transported to the ocean by way of this railroad and the Amoor.... With this railroad constructed, aside from the commercial views, the road would be highly valuable to Russia in the development and protection of her possessions on the Pacific coast...."

To finance his Amoor Railway Company, Collins proposed to raise most of the $20 million through the sale of stock, provided that the Russian government guaranteed at least seven percent of the total as well as the land, stone, wood, and iron rails for construction.

Collins spent four weeks in Nikolayevsk, anxiously awaiting a reply to his proposal. When one didn't come, he set sail for San

Wolfgang Kaehler

Francisco. Meanwhile, the Tsar's Siberian Committee was in the process of rejecting the proposal under the grounds that it was too expensive and difficult to complete. They sent a letter to Collins in San Francisco simply stating that the project was premature.

Despite their rejection of Collins's Siberian Railroad proposal, the Russian Tsarist government began encouraging people to migrate to the western regions of Siberia in an attempt to ease Russia's economic crisis and the growing discontent of the people. In addition, by 1870 many of the country's leading industrialists were searching for a way to exploit Siberia's natural resources. A steam-driven railway linking the north-south river systems was the best answer. Unfortunately, the huge landowners in western Russia were against such a railway, believing that wheat from the east would depress prices in the west. They also feared that the inevitable eastward migration in the event of such a railway would cause labor shortages in the west.

By the mid 1880s the industrialists won the sympathies of the new Tsar, Alexander III. This was the time of worldwide imperialism, and if Russia was to compete with other countries, Alexander felt it was necessary to open up Siberia and solidify Russian interests there. In addition, Alexander received numerous reports from Count Alexis P. Ignatyev, governor general of the Irkutsk province, stating that the Russian military positions in east-

ern Siberia would be highly susceptible to Chinese attack unless a railroad was completed between Irkutsk and Tomsk, providing supply lines and a method of moving troops.

Frustrated by his minister's lack of interest in a Siberian railway project, Alexander wrote: "How many times have I read such reports from the governors general of Siberia! I must own with grief and shame that up to the present the Government has done scarcely anything to meet the needs of this rich but forsaken country. It is time, it is high time!"

And high time it was. On March 29, 1891, Alexander III formed the Siberian Railway Commission to begin the planning and construction of the long-needed Trans-Siberian Railway. Alexander appointed his son and heir apparent, Nicholas, to oversee the project.

Nicholas proved to be a hardworking public relations agent and ambassador of goodwill. After lifting the first shovelful of dirt at Vladivistok in the spring of 1891, Nicholas traveled around Siberia drumming up support and enthusiasm for the project. The actual day-to-day planning and construction of the line was put in the hands of Finance Minister Sergius Yulyevich Witte. Born in Tiflis in 1848, Witte graduated from New Russian University in Odessa and subsequently joined the Odessa State Railway. After serving as traffic supervisor for fifteen years beginning in 1877, Witte was named Communications Minister in February 1892. By August of that year

When the railroad opened, the Russian press hailed it as "the fairest jewel in the crown of the Tsars." The always cynical British press, however, described it as "rusty streaks of iron through the vastness of nothing to the extremities of nowhere."

103

While the Trans-Siberian Railroad still enjoys a great deal of traffic, its tracks, locomotives, and rolling stock are antiquated and run down, even by today's low standards.

Wolfgang Kaehler

Alexander III named him Finance Minister and entrusted to him the entire Siberian Railway project.

Witte developed a timetable that divided construction into three stages . The West Siberian line, from Chelyabinsk to the Ob River; the Central Siberian line, from the Ob River to Irkutsk and Lake Baikal; and the Ussuri line, in eastern Siberia from Vladivostok to Khabarovsk, were all to be completed between 1894 and 1900. The second phase, the North Ussuri Line and the Transbaikal, from Lake Baikal to Srentensk, would begin construction in 1900, followed by the Circumbaikal loop, around Lake Baikal, and the Amur extension in phase three.

The initial stage of construction had a budget of $75 million, which included money for colonization, river improvements, and bridges for the Irtysh, Ob, and Yenisei rivers. Witte found an unexpected source of money when, at the prompting of Alexander, he formed a state liquor monopoly in an attempt to curb Russia's rising alcoholism rate. The monopoly failed at reducing liquor consumption, but it did raise a great deal of money. In the first year of the monopoly the government made nearly $12 million from liquor sales that averaged about three gallons for every man, woman, and child.

Wolfgang Kaehler

With finances at hand, construction of the eastbound track in West Siberia began on July 19, 1891, just outside Chelyabinsk. The chief engineer of the West Siberian sector was Constantine Ya Mikhailovski, the builder of the famed Alexander Bridge across the Volga River. Although much of the course followed flat plains, the region was prone to heavy frosts, limiting construction to about four months out of the year. Mikhailovski was also plagued by a shortage of building materials. Most of the sand, stone, and lumber in this section had to be shipped in from areas as far as 500 miles (800 kilometers) away. Another problem, which engineers of all sections of the Trans-Siberian Railway would face, was a shortage of skilled labor. Workers were recruited from Turkey, Italy, Persia, and western Russia. They slept in sod huts during the winter and tents during the summer, and suffered from a constant lack of food and medical supplies.

Despite the shortened work year, construction on this section went along quickly with few major problems. Considered one of the greatest civil engineers in Tsarist Russia, Mikhailovski completed the 900-mile (1,400-kilometer) section of track on August 30, 1895, at $700,000 below the estimated cost.

Construction of the Ussuri Line, the far eastern section of track, began on May 19, 1891 when Nicholas turned the first shovelful of dirt. Chief engineer Orest R. Vyazemski was entrusted with the job of pushing this 475-mile- (760-kilometer-) long line from Vladivostok, through the taiga, a swampy coniferous forest, onward to Khabarovsk.

Because of a shortage in local labor, Vyazemski was forced to use a combination of exiles, hard-labor prisoners, soldiers, and Chinese coolies. Each of these groups caused their own unique labor problems. The Chinese coolies had an obsessive fear of the Manchurian tiger. If a tiger was reported anywhere in the area, they refused to come out of their huts. The Chinese also refused to work in the rain.

The soldiers on the other hand, while they didn't mind working in the rain, didn't like working side by side with convicted criminals. Finding this demeaning, the soldiers worked slowly and took advantage of every chance they had to be taken off duty.

The exiles and criminals proved to be the most unruly group of the three. When not working, many of them spent their time terrorizing local citizens. The murder rate along the construction sites averaged nearly ten a week, and the robbery rate was so high nobody could keep track. The murder of a French naval officer at the hands of a rail worker led to a widespread protest demanding the removal of the worst of the criminals. Vyazemski was forced to comply, and the murder rate was lowered to one or two a week.

The thick, swampy taiga and heavy unexpected floods delayed construction even further. By 1894 only about 250 miles (400 kilometers) of track was laid, so Vyazemski sent a second work crew to Khabarovsk to begin work in the opposite direction. The Ussuri line was finally opened for service in November 1897.

The third line to be completed in the initial phase of the Trans-Siberian Railroad was the Central Siberian Section. In the summer of 1893, about the same time as Mikhailovski was pushing the Western line towards the Ob River, another work crew, under the leadership of chief engineer Nicholas R. Mezeninov, began cutting through the dense Siberian taiga from the Ob River to Irkutsk. Covering 1,148 miles (1,837 kilometers), this was the longest section of the railroad.

Mezeninov was inching his way through the swampy forests of birch, spruce, larch, and pine when word came from the Railroad Committee that the completion date had been moved up by two years. Mezeninov was working in an area that only had about three months of good weather during the year; the winter frosts didn't melt until the beginning of July and when they finally did thaw, they left the forest floor a virtual quagmire.

Mezeninov was able to solve the perpetual labor shortage by recruiting convicts from a prison near Irkutsk. These prisoners proved to be excellent workers—an ingenious incentive program reduced their sentences if they put in good work. All in all, Mezeninov had to house and feed more than 30,000 workers. According to published reports not one worker lost his life in an accident while building this line.

After the worst parts of the taiga were traversed, construction went along smoothly, and the Central Siberian railway was completed in August 1898, two years ahead of the original schedule. This was a remarkable feat considering that in one fifty-mile (eighty-kilometer) stretch more than eighty bridges had to be built.

In 1895, work began on the short forty-mile (sixty-four-kilometer) link between Irkutsk and the western bank of Lake Baikal as well as the Transbaikal railway from Mysovsk, just east of Baikal, to Srenensk, 687 miles(1,100 kilometers) away. Supplies had to be shipped from western Russia by sea, around Africa to the port of Vladivostok. From there they were transported up the then complete Ussuri line to Khabarovsk, where they were loaded onto riverboats and shipped up the Amur and Shilka Rivers. Construction of both of these sections was put in the hands of Alexander N. Pushechnikov. Fighting bitter winters, steep grades, and numerous rivers and canyons, Pushechnikov managed to finish these sections by January 1900.

Because of large mountains and rocky crags, the Circumbaikal section around the southern part of Lake Baikal was delayed until 1904. Up until then, trains were ferried across the lake in a huge, steam-powered boat.

The final irony of the entire Trans-Siberian saga is that the tsarist government that built the railroad never got to enjoy the fruits of its labor. The Bolsheviks inherited the railroad when they overthrew the tsar after World War I.

In the winter, when four-foot- (1.2-meter-) deep ice covered the lake, twenty miles (thirty-two kilometers) of track was laid directly on the ice, using large snowshoelike ties.

The Circumbaikal section that was eventually completed was one of the most difficult railroad engineering feats ever accomplished. More than thirty-three tunnels and 200 bridges and viaducts had to be constructed in the 160-mile (250-kilometer) section. Looping around crags and over ravines, this section was completed in September 1904.

In 1894, Sergius Witte received discouraging news from surveys conducted in the Shilka and Amur valley. Much of the 1,200-mile (1,900-kilometer) Amur River line that would connect the Transbaikal and the Ussuri lines just north of the Chinese border passed through ravines and river valleys. The line would require extensive cuttings, tunnels, and more than one hundred bridges, not including the two mile- (three kilometer-) long bridge needed to cross the Amur at Khabarovsk. The surveys went on to report that the railway could take a much more direct route through Chinese territory in Manchuria.

Meanwhile, in the summer of 1894, the Japanese had attacked China and soundly defeated her. As part of the peace settlement, Japan demanded substantial sections of Manchuria. Soon after the peace treaty was signed the Russians, backed by the French and Germans, intervened, threatening military actions against Japan unless it gave the Manchurian territories back to China. Rather than risk an all-out war, Japan relented, but it also demanded substantial payment from China in return.

Witte, realizing that China had no means of paying off such a huge war debt, arranged a 364-million-yen loan for China through the Paris Stock Exchange. In return, China agreed to the creation of the Chinese Eastern Railway linking the Trans-Siberian to the Russian port city of Vladivostok. While the ownership of the railway was under the name of the Chinese Eastern Railway Company, most of the stock in that company was owned by the Russian treasury. According to the contract, the railway would be turned completely over to the Chinese goverment after a term of eighty years.

Between the years 1897 and 1901, Russia spent huge sums of money trying to complete the Chinese Eastern Railway. Despite being plagued with the usual problems of labor and supply shortages, as well as epidemics and rough terrain, Russian engineers managed to push the railway towards completion by 1901. Certain political events, however, were to be the beginning of what would eventually cause the downfall of the Chinese Eastern Railway.

Between 1899 and 1901, fervent Chinese nationals began to rebel against the incursion of foreigners. The Boxer Rebellion began with the massacre of hundreds of Chinese Christians and foreign missionaries in 1899.

The rebellion eventually spread all over northern China with the passive support of the Chinese government and military. The rebellion was eventually crushed in 1901 when the combined forces of Japan, Britain, France, Germany, Russia, and the United States descended on Peking.

During the rebellion, the Chinese Eastern Railway sustained extensive damages. By the beginning of 1901, only about a third of the completed 800 miles (1,280 kilometers) of track was serviceable. Total damages were estimated at more than $35 million. As reconstruction work commenced, certain sections of the railroad were quickly opened. By November 1901, the entire railway was opened for local service; however, it was not until February 1903 that the rail system was declared fully operational. Twelve years after Nicolas turned the first shovelful of dirt, the Trans-Siberian Railway was open for uninterrupted service from Moscow to the distant Pacific port of Vladivostok. This incarnation of Russia's Finest Jewel was to be short-lived.

On February 9, 1904, the Japanese torpedoed Russian Naval units near Port Arthur, marking the beginning of the Russo-Japanese War. Port Arthur fell on December 20, 1904. This was followed by a Russian land defeat at Mukden in Manchuria and the crushing defeat of the Russian Navy in the Pacific. Pressured by these stunning losses and a growing revolutionary movement in European Russia, Nicholas II sought peace with the Japanese and eventually signed a peace treaty on September 5, 1905, at Portsmouth, New Hampshire, with United States President Theodore Roosevelt as mediator.

As part of the treaty, the Japanese retained control of Port Arthur, and the Chinese Eastern Railway was divided between the Japanese and the Russians. Russia eventually lost complete control and ownership of the Railway, leaving it without a complete Trans-Siberian link. In addition to its strain on the railway, the Russo-Japanese War marked a significant erosion of the tsar's power. Nicholas II reluctantly allowed the formation of the Duma, a national assembly, and fired many of his leading ministers, including Sergius Witte, the father of the Trans-Siberian Railway.

With their influence over Manchuria and eastern Siberia dwindling, Nicholas, with the prodding of new prime minister, P.A. Stolypin, decided to complete the missing Amur section of the railway between Chita and Khabarovsk. Using a massive work force of 80,000 men, mostly imported from European Russia, work was finally completed on this 1,200-mile (1,900-kilometer) section in 1916.

This final section of the Trans-Siberian cost one and a half times the total expenditures of the rest of the railroad combined (not including the Chinese Eastern Railway). Ironically, Russia spent the most money and resources on the one section it lost control of—the Chinese Eastern Railway cost $193 million, and

The Alaska Railroad was one of the most difficult rail-engineering feats ever attempted. Below, a steam locomotive pulls into the line's southern terminus at Seward, Alaska.

the Amur section cost $150 million. To further the irony, the Russian government that worked so hard and spent so much money to get this project completed never really enjoyed the fruits of its labor. The Trans-Siberian Railroad, and all of its potential, became the spoils of the Bolshevik Revolution, when the tsar was overthrown, at the end of World War I.

The Alaska Railroad

On March 30, 1867, Tsar Alexander II of Russia sold the 590,000-square-mile (1,528,100-square-kilometer) Alaska Territory to the United States for the paltry sum of $7,200,000, or roughly $12.20 per square mile. Since then Alaska has provided an invaluable source of oil and food for the United States. A major part of the economic success in the early period of Alaska's ownership by the United States and its transformation into statehood can be attributed to the development of the Alaska Railroad.

The first idea for a railroad through Alaska came at the beginning of the twentieth century when a group of businessmen in New York proposed a rail link between New York and Paris. The plan was to lay tracks from the western end of the Canadian Pacific Railroad at Port Rupert, north through Alaska, and then under the Bering Strait through a series

of tunnels. The line would then move south through eastern Russia and hook up with the Siberian Railway. The Railroad, which never went past the initial planning stages, would have connected New York, Toronto, Montreal, Moscow, Warsaw, Berlin, and Paris.

While this project never got off the ground, it did bring attention to the need for a railroad to exploit the natural resources of Alaska. Theodore Roosevelt was the first United States president to push for an Alaskan railroad; however, the binding restrictions of the Homestead Act of 1898 made such a project difficult. Alaska was officially named a United States territory with the passing of the Home Rule Act on August 24, 1912. Along with Alaska's new status came the appointment of the Alaska Railroad Commission. Members of the Commission included: William Edes, former chief engineer of the Northern Pacific Railroad; Colonel Frederick Mears of the United States Army, who worked on both the Great Northern and the Panama Canal Railroads; Thomas Riggs, an Alaskan surveyor and, later, the first governor of Alaska; Jay J. Morrow, the future Governor of the Panama Canal Zone; Leonard Cox, a United States Navy engineer; Dr. Alfred Brooks, vice-chairman of the United States Geological Survey; and Colen Ingerson, a railroad engineer.

On March 12, 1914, Woodrow Wilson signed the Alaska Railroad Act, which allotted

FPG International

Library of Congress

a maximum of $35 million for the surveying and construction of the railroad. Surveying teams headed by Edes, Mears, and Riggs traveled through the rough subarctic terrain and finally settled on two possible routes: one from the port of Valdez along the Tonsina and Delta rivers, northward through the Tanana River Valley to Fairbanks; the other from Seward, through the Nenia Peninsula, north along the Susitna Valley and then along the Nenana and Tanana Rivers on to Fairbanks.

In contrast to the surveyors on the Trans-Siberian and Canadian Pacific Railways, the Alaskan survey team worked with a great deal of efficiency and thoroughness. All of the survey work was completed on schedule by October 1914. Edes, Riggs, and Mears traveled to Washington, D.C., in February 1915 and presented maps, eyewitness reports, and geological surveys to President Wilson for the final decision. Three months later Wilson chose the more western route from Seward to Fairbanks through the Susitna Valley.

As part of the construction costs, the Alaska Railroad would buy two already existing railroads in Alaska: the Alaska Northern, which became an integral part of the new rail-road, and the Tanana Valley Railroad, a narrow gauge line that was in severe disrepair.

In an effort to avoid the death and disease that plagued workers on the recently completed Panama Canal and Railroad, Wilson urged that a great deal of consideration be given to employee health and welfare. Ample food and medical supplies were made available and the working conditions were strictly monitored. In addition, the workers were paid relatively high wages of about one hundred dollars a month, plus room and board. This unusual concern for the average worker ensured an ample supply of labor for the project. The small base camp at an area known as Ship Creek quickly grew into a town of about 2,000 hopeful workers. In July 1915, three months after the first spike was driven in, marking the beginning of construction, the residents of Ship Creek settlement voted to change the town's name to Anchorage.

Between the beginning of construction on April 29, 1915 and the outbreak of World War I, more than 100 miles (160 kilometers) of track were laid and put into operation. While the war did cause a slight labor shortage, the railroad did retain enough workers to keep construction going at a fairly con-

Because of drifting snow, sheds had to be built over some of the more mountainous sections of the Alaska Railroad.

109

The Alaska Railroad enjoys the distinction of being the only railroad in the United States that has been owned and operated by the Federal Government since its inception. One of the main attractions of the railroad is its glass-topped observation train.

stant pace. By this time, however, the three heads of the project were no longer involved in construction. Frederick Mears was called to service in Europe, Thomas Riggs resigned to become governor of Alaska, and William Edes became ill and was no longer able to carry out day-to-day duties. The project was then taken over by Panama Canal veteran William Gerig until the end of the war, when Mears returned to Alaska.

Although the railroad went nearly $20 million over budget, it was completed on schedule by July 1923. In a well-publicized ceremony, President Warren G. Harding, the first American president to travel to Alaska, drove in the final gold spike on July 15, 1923. Unfortunately, Harding fell ill on his return trip and died on August 2 in a hospital in San Francisco.

In a little over eight years, workers laid 522 miles (835 kilometers) of track through terrain where temperatures routinely reached seventy below in the winter and snow sometimes piled up into fifteen- to twenty-foot (five- to six-meter) drifts. The line also contains one of the world's longest single-span rail bridges, a 700-foot (213-meter) span across the Tanana River. One unique problem that the railroad still faces today is caused by the Alaskan moose. In the winter, snow creates steep twenty-foot (six-meter) piles on either side of the track. Moose sometimes stumble down the high snow banks and can't get back out. The trains are then forced to follow

the wayward moose miles down the tracks until the banks are low enough for them to escape.

Despite fairly constant traffic, the railroad did not register a profit for nearly twenty years. During World War II the Alaskan Railroad provided a vital supply link to the war-beleaguered Soviet Union. Because of its newly found strategic importance, the Alaska Railroad enjoyed a multimillion-dollar rehabilitation beginning in 1947. Potentially dangerous curves were straightened and rickety wooden bridges were replaced by new state-of-the-art steel spans. Since that time the railroad showed a steady increase in profits.

On March 27, 1964, Good Friday, tragedy struck Alaska and its railroad. The largest earthquake ever recorded in the Western Hemisphere rocked the territory. More than one hundred people were killed and thousands were injured. Massive tidal waves followed the earthquake, virtually wiping out a number of coastal settlements. Damage to the railroad alone was estimated at around $26 million. In a remarkable effort to get the railroad working again and, in turn, open Alaska back up for emergency medical aid, work crews had rail service restored within three weeks.

Today the railroad remains a valuable transportation and communications link to Alaska. It is the only major railroad in the United States that has been owned and operated by the Federal Government since its inception.

CHAPTER SIX

THE ADVENT OF ELECTRIC AND DIESEL LOCOMOTION

AT THE BERLIN EXHIBITION OF 1879, A GERMAN EN-gineer named Werner von Siemens demonstrated the first working electric rail locomotive. Making use of Michael Far-aday's discovery that electricity could create continuous mo-tion, Siemens powered thirty people around a circular track in a miniature locomotive. The three horsepower engine drew a low-voltage DC current through a live third rail; the train was able to travel four miles (six kilometers) per hour.

Although very primitive and slow, subsequent adaptations of this engine were later used in mining operations in the United States and Germany. Electric locomotives were per-fect for the mining industry. Their mechanical simplicity and the fact that they were not powered by any form of com-bustion made them dependable and safe for underground use.

Aside from use in the mining industry, early electric loco-motives were primarily used for urban trolley cars and ele-vated trains. In 1884, an electrical engineer named F.J. Sprague adapted the New York Elevated Railway to electric-ity. Later, while electrifying the Chicago "El" trains, Sprague invented the first multiple-unit (MU) trains, similar to those

Electric locomotion was the perfect answer for urban commuter trains. In the early days of the New York subway, there was a special car reserved for women only, and the fare was a nickel. Poor visibility from smoke and steam in the tunnels outside of New York's Grand Central Station (opposite page) caused several train collisions in the early 1900s. A public outcry led to the electrification of those tunnels.

used on today's subways and commuter trains. In this type of setup, each car is self-powered and controlled from a small cab in the front car. This eliminated the need for a large locomotive up front and made all electric rail cars interchangeable.

One year after Sprague electrified the New York El, a Belgian sculptor turned electrical engineer named Charles van Depoele perfected overhead wire transmission. This development made it possible to use high-voltage AC power without the dangers posed by a live third rail. By using high-voltage power, much longer trips were now possible.

Just a little over ten years after Siemens displayed his miniature electric locomotive, nearly 300 electric tramway systems were either under construction or being planned in the United States. Electric traction was perfect for urban transportation. It was quick, dependable, and much cleaner than steam-driven locomotives. City dwellers no longer had to suffer the black clouds of cinder-laden exhaust blowing through their streets. By 1906, most of the New York Elevated trains were moved underground into today's current subway system.

As the number of urban tramways grew, the larger mainline railroads began to look into the use of electricity for some of their underground links. The many long tunnels that were built under cities and through mountains posed severe problems for the smoke-spewing steam locomotives. The thick black exhaust impaired the vision of the engineer and choked the breath away from crewmen and passengers alike.

On July 27, 1895, the Baltimore & Ohio made history when it used a thirty-four-foot (ten-meter) electric locomotive to pull a standard steam train (locomotive and all) through the Howard Street tunnel in Baltimore, Maryland. This was by far the largest and most powerful electric locomotive of the day, and it opened the door for further use of the new technology by freight and passenger railroads. Up until this time electric trains were thought to be quick and dependable but not very powerful. This huge electric locomotive had the capability of towing a fully-loaded freight train, steam locomotive and all.

In January 1902, poor visibility from smoke and steam caused a catastrophic train collision under the streets of Manhattan just outside Grand Central Station, killing fifteen people. There had been a number of mishaps

The MU, or multiple-use train, was developed by electrical engineer F.J. Sprague for use on the Chicago "El" trains. The reliable MU train quickly became a standard for countries with rapidly growing mass transit systems. Right: Trains lie idle in a New York City subway train yard. Below top: a Bay Area Rapid Transit, or BART, train pulls into a station in the San Francisco area. Below bottom: a MARTA (Metropolitan Atlanta Regional Transit Authority) train.

Nikolay Zurek/FPG International

© Dean Abramson

© Stephen Varone/Envision

The Baltimore & Ohio Railroad was one of the first standard lines to put an electric locomotive into regular use. This battery-powered locomotive (below) was used to pull trains through a 7,300-foot (2,190-m) tunnel under the city of Baltimore. The electrification of the Pennsylvania Railroad up through New Jersey and into New York City led to the building of New York's Penn Station, one of the most beautiful railroad stations ever built.

in the same tunnel; however, this final deadly collision sparked a public outcry that led to the passage of a law prohibiting the use of steam engines in Manhattan after July 1, 1908.

The New York Central electrified all of its Manhattan lines using a low-voltage third rail system by 1906. One year later the New York, New Haven & Hartford became the first true mainline to electrify. Using a high-voltage, overhead transmission system, this new electric intercity train could reach top speeds of sixty miles per hour. Upon entering Manhattan, and the New York Central's low-voltage lines, the New Haven trains retracted their overhead connectors and lowered the electric "shoes" that hooked up with the third rail. This conversion from AC to DC was controlled by a switch in the conductor's box while the train was still moving. The electrification of New Haven's mainline system was so successful that the commuter railroad soon electrified all of its branch lines as well. The swift and efficient trains of the New York, New Haven & Hartford gave other heavily traveled commuter lines a reason to convert to the "juice." Within a few years, hundreds of conversions across the country were either planned or under way.

The New York, Westchester & Boston line was the first, and one of the few, railroads that was built as an electric line from the start. This commuter line serviced the northern suburbs of New York, but, despite its name, never went anywhere near Boston. Completed in 1912, the NYW&B used the latest and most expensive technology available in electric traction. The swift, streamlined railroad ran extremely well, but the cost of construction was so high, and the area it covered so sparsely populated, that the NYW&B was forced to close down by the end of 1937. Most other electric commuter lines were built

to less-costly specifications and as a result were much more successful. These profitable lines included: the Reading Railroad's Philadelphia to West Trenton branch; the Illinois Central's commuter line out of Chicago; and the Delaware, Lackawanna & Western's branch from Hoboken to Dover, New Jersey.

During the 1930s the Pennsylvania Railroad began an ambitious electrification program that would eventually cover nearly 3,000 miles (4,800 kilometers) of track. The Pennsylvania Railroad's conversion was the most extensive the world had ever seen. Even though most of the construction took place during the Great Depression, the switch over to electricity proved very profitable. More than five hundred multiple-unit coaches carried millions of commuters through the Philadelphia, New Jersey, and New York area.

Mainline passenger and freight service, however, was still driven by steam locomotives. In its search for a powerful locomotive to provide electric passenger service from New York to Washington, the PRR turned to General Electric and the Baldwin Locomotive Works. The two companies answered the call with the streamlined GG-1, a powerful machine that could reach top speeds of more than one hundred miles (160 kilometers) per hour. On January 28, 1932, the first GG-1 made a test run from New York to Washington, carrying a trainload of political figures and celebrities. The record-breaking trip took a mere three hours and twenty minutes, nearly an hour quicker than the fastest steam locomotive.

Some electrification of the PRR had actually taken place before 1910 when the tunnels under the Hudson River were opened, thus eliminating the need for ferries to Manhattan. This electrification led to the building of New York's Penn Station, one of the most

An early, high-speed electric Pennsylvania Railroad train pulls into Pennsylvania Station in New York. Penn Station was eventually demolished in the 1960s to make room for the current Madison Square Garden.

magnificent railroad stations ever built. Penn Station was eventually demolished in the 1960s to build the current Madison Square Garden.

One other major railroad to undergo widespread electrification was the Chicago, Milwaukee, St. Paul & Pacific. Beginning in 1915, this railroad underwent a transition to electricity that would eventually make it the most extensive electric rail system in the nation. Yet, at the same time that the majority of the railroad industry seemed set on electricity as the wave of the future, a quite different advancement was taking place that would make steam traction obsolete—the evolution of the internal combustion engine.

Dawn of The Diesel Era

Although electric locomotives were powerful, fast, and efficient, there were two major problems that prevented a large number of railroads from converting. First was the initial high cost of conversion and power generation. The original railroad companies that converted to electricity generated their own power. Later, they began buying electricity from power agencies; however, the fixed cost remained high. Second, electric trains were somewhat inflexible. Wires had to be strung along every foot of track, including yards and switching stations. Because it wasn't always practical to run lines through small and congested rail yards and even some sections of track, electric locomotives had to be supple-

mented with steam-powered switching cars and branch trains.

What the railroad industry needed was a motive power that combined the flexibility and power of steam with the efficiency and durability of electricity: Enter the diesel engine.

Since the beginning of the twentieth century a few rail companies had experimented with using the internal combustion engine to power locomotives. These early attempts, however, used gasoline-fueled engines, which could generate enough power for heavy loads. A better alternative came from an invention by the German scientist Dr. Rudolph Diesel.

Diesel's internal combustion engine burned a lower grade of fuel and could produce more power with less maintenance than the gasoline engine. Diesel, himself, mysteriously disappeared while crossing the English Channel in 1913. It is believed that German agents threw him overboard to prevent him from selling his invention to the English government. Despite Diesel's untimely demise, both German and American companies were able to improve upon his design. In 1930, General Motors introduced a two-cycle diesel engine that was far more compact and powerful than any internal combustion engine to date. Eager to find a market for this new engine, General Electric took it to the railroads.

In 1933, both the Union Pacific and the Chicago, Burlington & Quincy railroads built lightweight, streamlined trains that made use of the latest in diesel technology. The success of these two trains forever changed the face of the American railroad industry. In Febru-

ary 1934, the Union Pacific unveiled its M-1000, a sleek, three-car train that could easily reach and maintain blistering speeds of more than 100 miles (160 kilometers) per hour. To introduce its new high-speed train, the Union Pacific sent it on a cross-country publicity tour that would end in Chicago at the 1934 Century of Progress exhibition.

On May 26, 1934, the same day that M-1000 exhibit opened, the Burlington's new diesel speedster, the *Pioneer Zephyr*, made a record-breaking jaunt from Denver to the exhibition site. The train completed the 1,000-mile (1,600-kilometer) trip in just over thirteen hours, maintaining an average speed of seventy-seven miles (123 kilometers) per hour. Not to be outdone, the Union Pacific sent its second diesel train, the M-1001, on a high-speed cross-country chase the following year. The six-car streamliner traveled from Los Angeles to New York in just under fifty-nine hours, smashing the previous cross-country record by fifteen hours.

Both the Zephyrs and the M-1000 series trains were extremely profitable for their owners. They provided the ultimate in trans-continental luxury service. Cocktail lounges, observation decks, dining cars, and elaborate sleeping accommodations aboard these art-

At the beginning of the twentieth century, Dr. Rudolph Diesel (left) developed an internal combustion engine that eventually had a profound effect on the railroad industry. On May 26, 1934, the diesel-powered **Pioneer Zephyr** *(below) made a record-breaking trip from Denver to the Century of Progress exhibition in Chicago, covering 1,000 miles (1600 km) in just over thirteen hours.*

deco speedsters made cross-country train travel faster and more enjoyable than ever. At a time when the public had an intense fascination with the future, these streamlined wonders gave the impression that the future had already arrived. The *Pioneer Zephyr* was even the inspiration for (and appeared in) the 1934 film *The Silver Streak*.

In some ways the future had arrived, for these first two diesel trains sparked an immediate revolution in train travel. Less than a year after the *Pioneer Zephyr* was unveiled, the Electromotive Division of General Motors, the company that made the diesel engines, received orders from both the Baltimore & Ohio and the Santa Fe Railroads. It was not long before the methodical conversion of nearly all American railroads from steam to diesel would begin.

American Association of Railroads

The No. 1000 of Central Railroad of New Jersey was the first diesel-electric locomotive placed in regular service in the United States and was used primarily as a switching train. The success of trains such as the **Pioneer Zephyr** *(opposite page left) and the* **Kansas City Zephyr** *led to the gradual conversion of nearly all American railroads from steam to diesel.*

To say that these new trains were diesel powered is actually only partly true. A more accurate description would be diesel-electric trains. The diesel engine in these trains was coupled to a generator of electrical current. The actual motive power then was accomplished through electric traction motors. The original prototypes converted the diesel power into a DC traction motor. Later advancements were made so that the more powerful AC current could be used.

The perfection of this diesel-electric engine by General Motors was quite arguably the most significant development in railroad technology since George Stephenson first steamed across Britain in the *Rocket*. Certainly it had the most far-reaching consequences for the railroad industry in the United States. These new engines were faster, more reliable, and cheaper to operate than any steam locomotive ever built. While the original diesel trains lacked the power for heavy-load haulage, subsequent improvements made diesels even more powerful than the bulky steam

Between 1940 and 1955, the number of diesel engines in the United States jumped from 100 to 25,000. By 1960, only a handful of steam engines remained in service. Little did the railroad companies know that electricity would eventually prove the most economical and efficient form of rail power.

haulers. Quite simply, the steam locomotive was becoming a thing of the past.

Between 1940 and 1955, the number of steam engines on American railroads dropped from 40,000 to 2,000. During the same period, the number of diesel engines shot up from about 100 to 25,000 and accounted for about 90 percent of all rail traffic in the country. A few railroads such as the Chesapeake & Ohio, the Norfolk & Western, and the Virginian, tried to resist the trend toward diesel, but by 1955 all had at least a few diesel trains operating on their tracks. By the mid 1960s, virtually all steam locomotives had either been dismantled or relegated to museum displays.

Europe Goes Diesel... Or Does It?

A similar conversion to diesel had been going on in Europe during the pre–World War II era. The most adamant backers of diesel power were the Germans. They, too, developed a group of high-speed streamliners similar to the American Zephyrs. The *Fliegende Kölner,* the *Fliegende Frankfurter,* and the *Fliegende Hamburger* each made daily commuter trips at speeds that regularly averaged between seventy and eighty miles (110 and 130 kilometers) per hour. France, Sweden, It-

aly, and Great Britain all had begun making the transformation to diesel when World War II broke out and aborted their projects.

Because of their strategic importance in providing supplies for the warring armies, the European railroads were hit extremely hard during World War II. Tracks were torn up, locomotives destroyed, rolling stock was burned, and terminals were bombed out. The French lost half of their locomotives and nearly 80 percent of their routes were at least partially destroyed. England had been riddled with bombs and little of its extensive rail system went unscathed. Germany had been defeated and subsequently divided. With the partitioning of the country, most of the German railroads were also divided.

The European rail system as a whole was almost completely devastated. Because of the rail's importance to European economy and communications, much of the reconstruction of Europe had to entail reconstruction of its railroads.

As Europe began to rebuild its railroads, the question of what form of traction to use again rose. Using newer technologies developed during the war, the French took the route of electrification. The new technology allowed for high-voltage AC power with fewer electrical substations and reduced installation costs. This seemed the most practical and economical way to go. Electrical traction could achieve quicker acceleration and better adhe-

© Marcus Brooke/FPG International

A crowded commuter train pulls into Central Station in Glasgow, Scotland (opposite page). European countries were much more reluctant to adopt the diesel than the United States. Switzerland's Gornergrat railroad (left) was one line that chose electric locomotion over diesel. A British Rail InterCity train (below) charges down the track.

sion than diesel power. In addition, its lower maintenance requirements put less of a strain on the fragile postwar French economy.

By 1955, 80 percent of the French railroads were using electric traction. Their new rail system was dependable, fast and efficient, and it quickly became the model for the rest of Europe's rail reconstruction. One by one, the other European countries rebuilt their systems using electric traction. In a little over fifty years the preferred technology for European railroads had switched from steam to electric to diesel and back to electric again. In America, on the other hand, the diesel revolution was still in full swing. Yet, while railroad optimists thought diesel was the future of American railroads, it was that very technology that ultimately led to its demise.

The Decline of The American Railroads

In one sense, the perfection of the internal combustion engine gave the American railroad companies the exact technology they were looking for—a fast and dependable motive power that was inexpensive to operate. Unfortunately for the railroad industry, the internal combustion engine and diesel technology also gave its competitors exactly what they were looking for. The diesel trucking industry was quickly becoming the country's chief mode for transporting goods. Trucks could do what trains could not—they could make shipments from door to door, anywhere in the country, and they were far less dependent upon schedules.

In addition, America's booming aviation industry was quickly depleting the railroad's

long-distance passenger service. No matter how fast a train was, the airplane was always faster. The fifties was also the decade of the car. Oil and gas were cheap and plentiful, and virtually everyone who was old enough to drive did. This shift to the automobile weakened the railroad industry's last remaining stronghold, commuter traffic.

By the 1960s, railroad profits had begun to plummet. The industry up to that time was a fragmented conglomeration of private companies. It had no governing organization and no real mechanism for working together. The European train systems survived much better, largely because they were state owned and had one governing body that could determine where to cut back and where to expand. The American system was based on competition, but while the railroad companies were competing among themselves, new competitors— the trucking and airline industries—snuck in and stole the show.

During the 1960s and 1970s, small railroad freight companies went out of business or were absorbed by the larger ones. The larger companies, in order to survive, either merged or were rescued by the government. In 1973, Congress passed the Rail Reorganization Act, creating the United States Railway Association in an attempt to resuscitate the dying rail-freight industry. One of its first actions was to establish the Consolidated Rail Corporation or Conrail, a government owned amalgamation of bankrupt rail systems.

Much of the nation's passenger rail service needed rescuing as well. In 1930, there were 15,000 daily long-haul passenger trains in the United States. By the 1970s that number had shrunk to 500, which were making very small, if any, profits. On April 30, 1971, the federal

By the late 1950s and early 1960s, the American railroad industry suffered from the increasing competition posed by the trucking, aviation, and automobile industries. In an attempt to save the flagging rail-freight industry, the federal government formed Conrail, a government-owned and operated rail system (left). Opposite page: Two vintage locomotives lie fallow in the B&O rail Museum in Baltimore, Maryland.

After World War II, the French led the way in railway electrification. Today, their TGV trains are among the fastest and most reliable passenger trains in the world.

government formed Amtrak, a federally subsidized corporation that would run a network of intercity passenger trains. While Amtrak did manage to keep passenger rail service alive, especially in the always busy Northeast corridor, Conrail never really took hold. After operating millions of dollars in the red, the government withdrew virtually all of its support by the mid 1980s, effectively dismantling the struggling freight service.

The current American railroad industry is still alive, yet it faces many challenges, the most significant of which is the precarious state of the nation's tracks. Literally thousands of miles of tracks have not been repaired or aligned since they were originally laid. If the railroad industry is to survive, it must overhaul its tracks and invest in new high-speed electric trains. The railroad can still be a very valuable contributor to the nation's passenger and freight transport system; however, the days when the iron horse dominated the American landscape and economy are long gone and most likely will never be seen again.

High-Speed Travel

During the 1950s, inter-city passenger trains began to suffer from increased competition from other modes of transportation. Air travel was regarded as safe and fast. Planes had an added advantage because they were not limited by a network of iron rails; they could take off and land in virtually any major city in the world. In addition, the worldwide automotive industry was growing by leaps and bounds. A revitalized post-war economy meant that more and more people could afford cars, and given the choice between travelling on a sometimes unreliable passenger train and driving themselves, most people chose to drive.

In order to combat this growing competition, the passenger rail industry began to revamp their equipment to acquire higher speeds and better efficiency. The French were the pioneers in the development of high-speed rail travel. As part of their post-war redevelopment, the French built a fleet of first class high-speed trains aimed at the business market. The best known of these was the Paris-Lyon-Marseille-Nice 'Mistral', which covered the 195-mile (312-kilometer) distance at an average speed of more than eighty miles (128 kilometers) per hour.

These new trains were a great success, prompting the French to make even larger inroads into high-speed travel. In March 1955, the French unveiled and tested two new 4,000 horsepower trains on a stretch of track near Bordeaux. The first train, No. CC 7107, easily hit a speed of 171.5 miles (274 kilometers) per hour. Two days later, its companion train, BB9004, hit a record-shattering speed of 205.6 miles (329 kilometers) per hour.

First introduced on the Paris-Lyon line, the TGV trains work efficiently at 125 miles (200 km) per hour and can hit top speeds of more than 160 miles (256 km) per hour.

Although breaking the 200-mile- (320-kilometer-) an-hour barrier was a remarkable feat in railroad engineering, it was done under optimum, controlled conditions. Two-hundred-mile- (320-kilometer-) an-hour travel was still not practical for day-to-day operations. Yet, the French speed trials did prove that inter-city rail travel at more than 100 miles (160 kilometers) per hour was possible. After ten years of technological improvements on virtually every train component—from the wheels, to electrical conductors, to tracks—the French introduced the TGV on their Paris-Lyon line. The new TGV trains worked efficiently at 125 miles (200 kilometers) per hour and could hit top speeds in excess of 160 miles (256 kilometers) per hour. Today, the TGVs are still among the most reliable high-speed trains in the world.

Japan's Shinkansen, meaning New Railways, were part of a comprehensive plan for high-speed travel. The Japanese combined expensive, custom-built track with a high-speed "bullet" train. The space-age design of these sleek trains is a far cry from George Stephenson's primitive "Rocket."

While the French were the first to test and experiment with high-speed trains, the Japanese were the first to prove that day-to-day rail operations at more than 100 miles (160 kilometers) per hour was mechanically feasible. To do it, however, they had to lay a custom-built railway designed specifically for the purpose. In October 1964, the Japanese government unveiled the New Tokaido Line between Tokyo and Osaka. This was the first of Japan's Shinkansen ('New Railways'), widely known across the world as bullet trains.

Originally, the New Tokaido line was to be used for nighttime freight service as well as daytime passenger service, but eventually freight service was dropped. Soon after the line opened it became evident that the entire railway would have to be shut down for six hours every night for maintenance to the track and catenary system. Despite this need for daily maintenance, the Shinkansen set a world standard for efficiency and economic performance. By 1969, eight trains traveled each way everyday on the New Tokaido, carrying more than a half million people at an average speed of 101 miles (162 kilometers) per hour, reaching a top speed of 130 miles (208 kilometers) per hour.

© Paul Chesley/Photographers Aspen

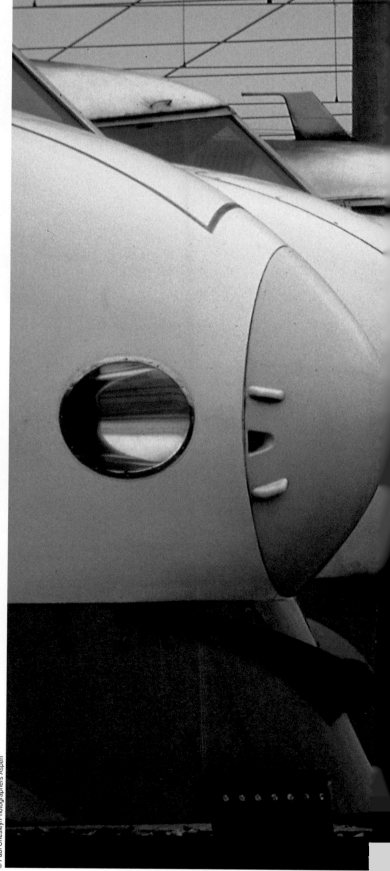

© Paul Chesley/Photographers Aspen

© Michael J. Howell/Envision

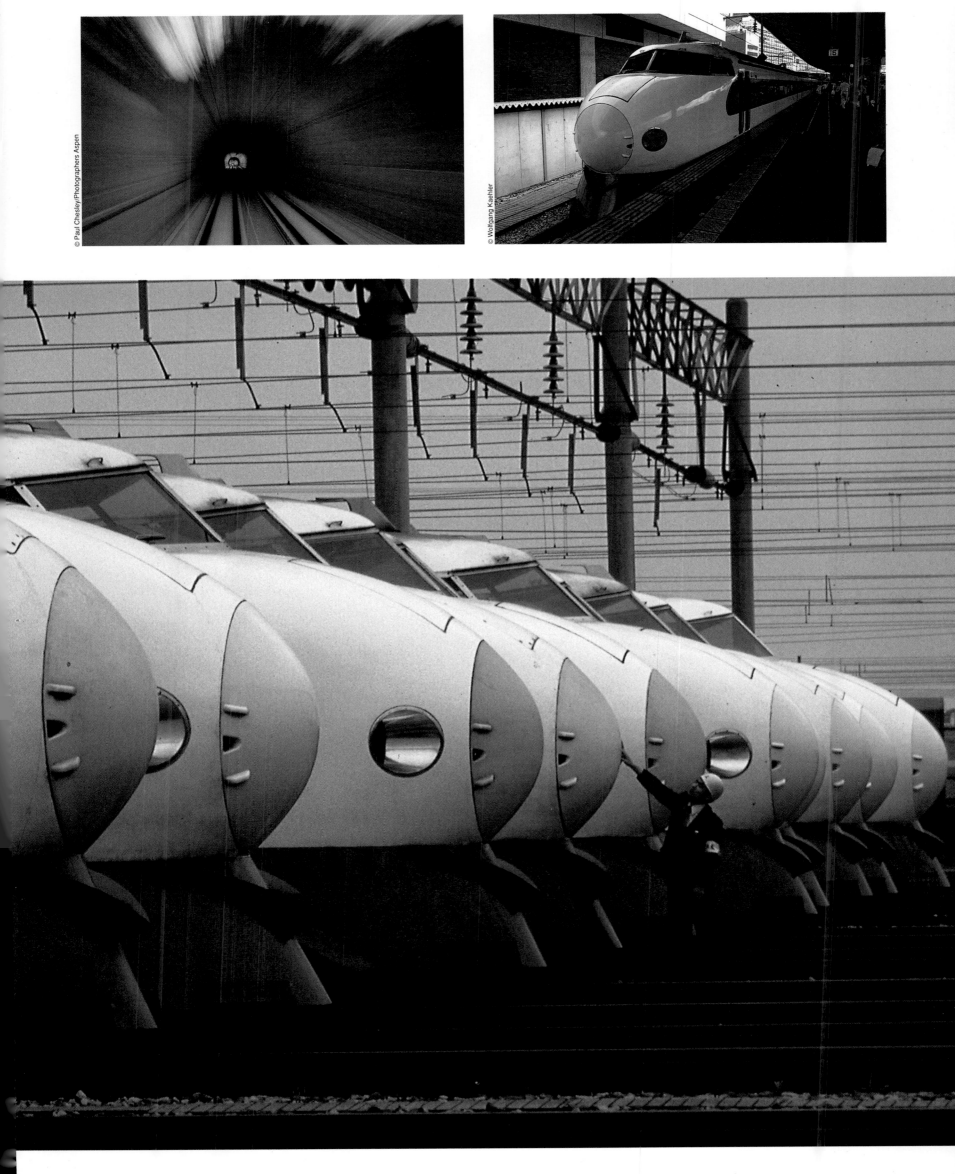

© Dean Abramson

The original plan called for trains that could maintain a top speed of 160 miles (256 kilometers) per hour. This speed, however, was much faster than the dilapidated track in the northeast corridor could handle. In addition, the Metroliners were based on technology that had gone largely untested. Metroliner service finally began in 1971 under the auspices of Amtrak—four years late and hundreds of thousands of dollars over budget.

Despite early problems, the Metroliner has become the most economically successful of all Amtrak trains. Averaging speeds in excess of 90 miles (144 kilometers) per hour it remains the closest thing to the Japanese Shinkansen in the United States. Still, despite the proven successes of high-speed train travel around the world, the United States seems unwilling to make a major commitment toward expanding its inter-city passenger service; the costs of track improvements alone would cost hundreds of millions of dollars. Yet, in order to preserve the age-old tradition of rail travel between major cities, some sort of improvements are necessary.

The development of the Shinkansen trains had a profound impact on the passenger train industry in the United States. In September 1965, President Lyndon Johnson signed the High Speed Ground Transportation Act authorizing the development of a high-speed passenger train between Boston, New York, and Washington. The new United Aircraft Turbotrains became known as the Metroliners. From the beginning the Metroliners were plagued with technical problems.

In 1965, President Johnson signed the High Speed Ground Transportation Act authorizing the development of "Metroliner" service between Boston, New York, and Washington. The Metroliner remains the most economically viable of all passenger lines in the United States. Above: A revamped Union Station in Washington, D.C.

© Dean Abramson

With the formation of Amtrak, the United States government hoped to save the country's ailing inter-city passenger train service. Still dependent on government funding, Amtrak has yet to stand on its own.

© Mark Gibson

Amtrak is gradually being weaned from government funding. Only time will tell if the passenger rail company will be able to survive on its own.

© Ernst H. Robl

Bibliography

Allen, G. Freeman, *Railroads: Past, Present, and Future.* London: Orbis Publishing, Ltd, New York: William Morrow and Co, New York, 1982.

———————— , *Railways the World Over.* New York: Philosophical Library, 1957.

Barsley, Michael, *The Orient Express: the Story of the World's Most Fabulous Train.* New York: Stein and Day Publishers, 1967.

Beebe, Lucius M., *Mr. Pullman's Elegant Palace Car: The Railway Carriage that Established a New Dimension of Luxury and Entered the National Lexicon as a Symbol of Splendor.* Garden City, N.Y.: Doubleday, 1961.

Buder, Stanley, *Pullman: an Experiment in Industrial Order and Community Planning, 1880–1930,* New York: Oxford University Press, 1967.

Fitch, Edwin M., *The Alaska Railroad.* New York: Frederick A. Praeger, Inc. 1967.

Elting, Mary, *All Aboard!: The Railroad Trains that Built America* [Rev. ed.]. New York: Four Winds Press, 1970, © 1969.

Haine, Edgar A., *Seven Railroads.* New York: A.S. Barnes & Co, 1979.

Hudson, F.K., editor, *Rail Book Bibliography, 1948–1972: A Comprehensive Guide to the Most Important Railbooks, Publications and Reports.* Ocean, New Jersey: Specialty Press, Inc. 1972.

Jacobson, Timothy, Photographs by Dudley Witney, *An American Journey by Rail.* New York: W.W. Norton & Co, 1988.

McCague, James, *Moguls and Iron Men: The Story of the First Transcontinental Railroad.* New York: Harper & Row, 1964.

McKee, Bill and George Klassen, *Trail of Iron: The CPR and the Birth of the West, 1880–1930.* Vancouver/Toronto: The Glenbow-Alberta Institute in association with Douglas & McIntyre, 1983.

Perkins, Harold, *The Age of the Railway.* New York: Drake Publishers, Inc. 1973.

Poor, Henry V., *History of the Railroads and Canals of the United States of America.* New York: A.M. Kelley, 1970.

Rando, John Francis and Robert Francis Rando, *The American Railroads.* Delaware City: J.F.R. Publishing House, 1970.

Rolt, L.T.C., *George and Robert Stephenson.* London: Longmans, 1960.

Sinclair, Angus, *Development of the Locomotive Engine.* Annotated ed. prepared by John H. White, Jr, Cambridge: M.I.T. Press, 1970, © 1907.

Smiles, Samuel, *The Life of George Stephenson, Railway Engineer.* Ann Arbor, Michigan: Plutarch Press, 1971.

Tupper, Harmon, *To the Great Ocean: the Taming of Siberia and the Building of the Trans-Siberian Railway.* Boston: Little, Brown & Company, 1965.

Weaver, John C., *The American Railroads,* Garden City, New York: N. Doubleday, 1958.

INDEX